To the co[...]

Keep return...

— Amy Dogan

10/30/23

Praise for
The Informational Interview Playbook

"In any industry they always say it's all about who you know and who knows you. Nobody understands that better than Henry Organ. A master in the art of cultivating relationships, Organ outlines his key strategies and personal insights for growing your professional or personal network. *The Informational Interview Playbook* is a must-read for anyone looking to level up in their career!"

Jory Zemanek

director of partnerships, BreakAway Data

"Mastering the informational interview is not only vital for your career success, it's a life skill and a sales skill, too. Connecting with busy people from whom you seek advice is like a superpower. This book gives you the step-by-step methodology, mindset, and marching orders to talk to almost anyone. If you want to generate more opportunities for your career, your business, and your life, follow every single step that Henry lays out in this masterful book."

David Newman

bestselling author, *Do It! Marketing* and *Do It! Selling*

"We've all heard the advice, 'it's who you know, not what you know,' but Organ's *Informational Interview Playbook* gives a direct intentional action plan to get those important connections that'll help you thrive in your career. I'd recommend this book for a young person seeking direction, those needing a career reboot, or anyone who needs to maximize relationships with those they want to emulate. Organ gives detailed practical examples of how a trio of steps—prep, execution, follow-up—can launch you to the next level. This book is an informative and entertaining read full of golden gems."

Cameron Wolfe

national TV reporter, NFL Network

"Henry Organ's journey is the epitome of hard work and grit. His approach to career building is something everyone can learn from, no matter where you are at in your journey."

Andy Miguel

senior vice president and head of marketing, Hyperice

"Young professionals looking for real-life examples, inspiration, and guidance across business development and personal growth, this is a book for you. Organ delivers career advice that will enhance your work-life trajectory."

Jeff Lulay

brand manager, Nike

"I've said for years that the idea of waiting for some imaginary perfect job listing to come across your screen is not the path to your dream job or your dream career. It's all about deciding where you want to work and who you want to work for. *The Informational Interview Playbook* is the secret weapon to actually making that happen, and now you can master it with this book."

Les Green

CEO, *SLAM Magazine*

www.amplifypublishing.com

The Informational Interview Playbook: Creating a Path to Achieve Your Career Goals

For more information, please contact:
Amplify Publishing, an imprint of Amplify Publishing Group
620 Herndon Parkway, Suite 220
Herndon, VA 20170
info@amplifypublishing.com

Library of Congress Control Number: 2023907941
CPSIA Code: PRV0623A
ISBN-13: 978-1-63755-624-5

Printed in the United States

For both of my late grandpas—

Dr. Claude Organ and Ed Devine.

For the lifelong learners—you will always succeed.

Henry Organ
with Cody Sims

The **Informational Interview Playbook**

Creating a Path to Achieve Your Career Goals

amplify
an imprint of Amplify Publishing Group

Contents

Foreword

As co-founder and CEO of Obsidianworks Creative, I have had the pleasure of knowing Henry Organ for more than ten years. *The Informational Interview Playbook: Creating a Path to Achieve Your Career Goals* is a blueprint on how to master the fundamentals of networking and career development so you are actively in control of your future.

I have watched how Henry navigated through the various spaces he references in this book. After all, I was one of the individuals he reached out to for an informational interview early in his career at Nike. I have had a front row seat to his journey and am proud of what Henry has accomplished already.

On a personal level, I can also attest that what Henry is saying works. I was at Nike for a little over a decade before I decided to start a marketing and creative company. Neither my time at Nike, nor my starting Obsidianworks Creative would have been possible without the various conversations that prepared me for where I am today. So as a person who has benefited from informational interviews myself, I understand the importance of understanding not only how to have them, but how to master them.

This book is created for those with a growth mindset and a desire to achieve beyond what they think is possible. It offers clear instructions and straight talk—just like its author—while also enlightening and inspiring. It isn't meant to just be read once and put on a bookshelf. Instead, this should be used as an interactive workbook providing you with necessary tools to grow and develop. So grab your pen or pencil; you're going to need it.

Chad Easterling
Co-founder and CEO of Obsidianworks Creative

Introduction

"Create a vision of who you want to be,
and then live into that picture as if it were
already true."
Arnold Schwarzenegger

Getting Started

This book is your personal playbook to getting ahead in life. Whether you are looking to find your true purpose or to flourish in the journey you are already on, mastering informational interviews can be the catalyst to help you reach your desired goals and the vision you have for yourself. Without implementing informational interviews, you will waste countless days, months, and even years without living up to your full potential. While it's admirable to have a "can do" attitude at times, it is important to recognize that you do not have to figure out *everything* on your own. In fact, you are doing yourself a huge disservice by not learning from other people's experiences. I'd go as far as saying you'd be a fool not to take full advantage of the blueprints others are happy to share with you. Having tactical conversations can help you gain clarity faster, avoid potential mishaps throughout your career and life, and create opportunities that you may not be able to conjure up alone. There's no need to reinvent the wheel.

Why am I so confident that informational interviews can be this influential in creating the life you want to live? I've personally had over 100 informational interviews, and they got me where I am today. From landing my first corporate job at Nike World Headquarters in Football Brand Marketing to becoming an NFLPA-certified agent and co-founder of Disruptive Sports Agency to closing on my first property my first year out of undergrad to closing on my first investment property while in grad school in one of the most competitive markets in the world, I credit a great deal of my early success to strategic informational interviews. I don't say this to brag or boast, but rather to shed light on how informational interviews played such an integral role in both accelerating my career and reaching personal milestones sooner than I had ever dreamed possible.

I discovered the power of informational interviews from a guy I met who worked at Nike HQ, Ian Williams. At the time, I was fresh out of college and working at the Nike employee retail store, trying to figure out how I could land a job at Nike HQ. Ian was one of my first informational interviews—before I even knew what an informational interview was.

Ian always wanted to work at Nike. He didn't get his college degree and he didn't really know what he wanted to do besides work at Nike. He took a job as a janitor at Nike HQ and happened to meet a Nike developer. He ended up having an informational interview discussing what the developer's role was. When they finished up the informational interview, Ian asked the developer if he needed any help. Ian was looking to provide value in any way that he could. The developer happened to need help organizing all the shoes in the Nike development building.

Ian knew if he was in the right environment for a certain period of time and worked hard, he would get an opportunity. Ian was courageous enough to ask the team at Nike Skateboarding (SB) if he could design a shoe, and they actually ended up letting him. He designed the Nike Dunk High SB Wet Floors—a bold yellow, black, white, and red shoe incorporating colors that were inspired by his time as a janitor. Three years later Ian got a formal interview for a footwear developer position and landed the job. After five years working in that role, he realized he no longer wanted to work behind a desk. He loved interacting with people and everything that makes up the sneaker community. He eventually opened up a sneaker-themed coffee shop, Deadstop Coffee in Portland, Oregon. Ian went from being a janitor to a shoe developer to eventually a business owner.

Ian played a pivotal role in helping me realize that informational interviews have the potential to land me jobs, create business opportunities, and even change my life. Ian also gave me other useful tips that I will elaborate throughout the book. Using Ian's method as a lighthouse to guide me, I was able to refine my informational interview skills through trial and error. Like anything, the more informational interviews I did, the more they improved. I became diligent about taking detailed notes.

Luckily, early in my career Ian taught me the importance of having informational interviews the right way. I get tons of calls from students who are curious about what it takes to become a sports agent. Surprisingly, within thirty seconds of almost every conversation I have, the person shows me that they have not done their research on who I am or what the prerequisites are to becoming an agent. When people have not done their due diligence prior to a call, it signifies that the person lacks clarity; they may even be incapable of obtaining an entry-level position. It's okay to ask questions; it's not okay to be unprepared. Mastering informational interviews will teach you how to stay in the know and advance your career.

Whether it be applying for jobs or running a company, traditional ways that once worked no longer seem to. I understand it can be extremely frustrating trying to make your mark in what can feel like an ever-changing landscape. But change is inevitable across all industries. Events beyond our control, rapidly evolving technology, and overall competition may seem like a recipe for disaster, but I'm here to tell you, those things are here to stay. Since challenges will always be present, you need to learn how to grow and adapt even in what may seem like chaos. Despite it all, you can win. I want to help you get ahead of the curve not only in your career, but in life.

What initially sparked my interest in writing this book was the fact that a resource like this would have been a lifesaver when I was first getting acquainted with informational interviews. Hell, I didn't even know what an informational interview was. Once I discovered the power of informational interviews and saw how much they helped me, I simply couldn't be a gatekeeper withholding this information. This book can transform your life, no matter where you are starting from or what your second-grade teacher or your college professor said you couldn't do.

A Heads-Up

At times throughout this book I will be extremely direct with you. I will shoot you straight because there comes a point in your life when you have to be brutally honest with yourself. Sometimes it takes an outsider being ultra direct to cut through the clutter and get you to wake the fuck up. Sometimes it takes someone directly asking you thought-provoking questions to get you to idle long enough to come up with an answer. And not someone else's answer—yours.

In our world of "go, go, go," you can drive yourself crazy if you are going in the wrong direction. Sometimes we must slow down in order to evaluate and accelerate in the right direction. Sometimes we get so in the weeds with our day-to-day activities, we forget the importance of taking a birds-eye view of our life too. Not only will I give you practical advice, but throughout the book I will also ask that you be okay with thinking outside the box and staying open to new ideas. You'll be surprised by what embracing a different vantage point can do for you.

From this point on, choose a growth mindset. My grandpa had a phrase he would constantly say to me and probably everyone else he knew: "I'm not about the bull-shit!" I used to think it was just a funny phrase, but now I realize how serious he actually was. He wasn't about the bullshit because he knew he couldn't afford to be screwing around and not taking his life seriously. My wish for you is that you adopt that same mentality. This is not a drill. This is not a test drive. You have a limited amount of time on this earth, and I want you to capitalize on every fuckin' minute. We forget that we have unlimited potential, and that we can inspire others to strive for theirs. However, in order to create an everlasting impact, we must first focus on being the best version of ourselves.

More often than not, people will blame others or incidents that have occurred throughout their lives as the reasons they never reach their goals. Let me tell you, everybody's got a sob story. What's important is that you wake the fuck up and realize you can still win, even when the odds are stacked against you! Growing up I was diagnosed with ADHD and dyslexia. In elementary school, I would try to hide during reading time just so the teacher wouldn't call on me. There were countless times I felt embarrassed, berated, and told I would never amount to anything. Despite it all, I had a strong sense of self from my parents and grandparents, who taught me that I could do anything I set my mind to. Eventually, I realized that with persistence and planning anything is possible. The more often you can make a game plan and consistently execute, the luckier you will get. The world will reward you for striving for your purpose unapologetically. I'm just here to help you get there faster.

A Personal Request

At the end of each chapter, I've included an "Apply It" section. After reading each chapter, it's crucial that you take a time-out to answer each of the questions to get the most out of this book. When I say answer the questions, I mean write your answers down. I challenge you to take a pragmatic approach and take your time when reflecting on each question. Some of the questions will require more introspection than others. If you scurry around the questions, the only person you're cheating is yourself.

People always say "knowledge is power," but that phrase is oftentimes misconstrued. Knowledge is power if and only if you learn to apply the knowledge you've gathered in your everyday life. All the books, seminars, and pep talks will do absolutely nothing for you if you do not actively take the time to put the acquired knowledge into practice. Now let's create the life you want to live! It's time to get to work.

Part I

The Prep

Chapter 1

What Is an Informational Interview?

"Never be afraid to learn something,
because the moment you stop learning is
the moment you start dying."
Albert Einstein

I f you picked up this book, you most likely want to accomplish more. Before you read any further, you must be willing to truly commit to being open-minded and implementing what you learn to garner the results you're seeking. In order to get what you've never gotten, you must do what you've never done. In life there will never be any free handouts, at least not any that will be life-changing. In a world that constantly wants a dose of instant gratification, the biggest paradox in life is that in order to accomplish true success and ultimate gratification, you must be willing to put in the work.

While there's no magic potion or get-rich-quick scheme that actually works, there are strategies you can use to reach your goals faster. In this book, I will teach you how to cultivate the life you want by mastering informational interviews to propel you forward.

What can you do to give yourself an edge to get ahead and gain more traction in whatever your passion may be? How can you gain pertinent information in any industry during the ebbs and flows of your professional career? It really all boils down to one thing—establishing more connections.

By utilizing informational interviews to establish more connections, you can grow exponentially regardless of what stage of your career you're in. Fresh out of college and looking to secure your first job? Have more informational interviews. Unhappy in your current job and curious about pivoting into a totally different field or want to get a promotion? Have more informational interviews. Are you a business owner looking to grow your company but cannot seem to break out of a plateau? You guessed it, have more informational interviews.

You are probably thinking, "That all sounds good, Henry . . . but what the hell are informational interviews?!" An informational interview is a great way to learn about how somebody got to where they are so you can connect the dots. According to UC Berkeley, an informational interview is "an informal conversation you can have with someone working in an area of interest to you. It is an effective research tool and is best done after preliminary online research." * By having informational interviews, you can take elements of someone's story to figure out how to advance your career or accomplish an objective.

You can read a plethora of "how-to" books, but until you talk to the person who is where you want to be, your desired career path may seem out of reach. Having numerous informational interviews allows you to essentially get a road map to a destination you've never been to before.

When informational interviews are discussed, they are usually spoken about in an elusive manner. Sometimes people will encourage you to get out there and "network." If you're looking for a job, they'll tell you to "apply online." Unfortunately, that's usually where the advice stops. Advice without practicality is fluff. No wonder you get frustrated.

It's becoming virtually impossible to get ahead in any career or even land an entry-level position by solely "applying online." I know the story all too well; it used to be me getting denied for the numerous positions I applied for. I'd apply to jobs daily, hoping to get a response. Best-case scenario, I would get an email politely letting me know they were going in another direction. The email would read: "Mr. Organ, We're sorry. Although you have impressive qualifications, we have decided to move forward with other candidates at this time. We will keep you in mind for other opportunities in

---

* https://career.berkeley.edu/start-exploring/informational-interviews

the future that you may be a good fit for." At first I would get upset. Then I began to wonder if my applications were even being opened. The overall process and automated email responses seemed like complete and utter BS.

After thorough research, I began to realize maybe there was some truth to what I was thinking. According to a job search services firm, Indeed, about 75 percent of all job applications never reach human eyes for review.[*] Applicant tracking systems scan and automatically weed out around three-fourths of all applicants. In addition, recent research reported as much as 80 percent of jobs in the entire US are filled by personal and professional connections[†]. Furthermore, Matt Youngquist, Founder of Career Horizons, stated that roughly 70 percent of all jobs never even get published on job sites.[‡] Shit!!

So, if the odds are statistically stacked against you, how do you succeed? You should use these stats as both insight and encouragement. You have to think of ways to stand out. Whether you are trying to land a job or looking to make fruitful connections in your business, the bottom line is people like to do business with people they know personally or are somehow already connected to.

---

[*]   https://www.indeed.com/career-advice/finding-a-job/quality-vs-quantity-applications

[†]   https://www.cnbc.com/2019/12/27/how-to-get-a-job-often-comes-down-to-one-elite-personal-asset.html#:~:text=Research%20shows%20that%2070%25%20of,career%20only%20stands%20to%20grow

[‡]   https://www.npr.org/2011/02/08/133474431/a-successful-job-search-its-all-about-networking

You'll frequently hear people say successful people only got to where they are because of nepotism. Considering the stats I noted above, that may be partially true. Let's take a closer look at the definition of "nepotism." The *Oxford English Dictionary* defines nepotism as, "The practice among those with power or influence of favoring relatives or friends, especially by giving them jobs." Sure, if someone is über-successful in their career, they've also had to do the work once they got their foot in the door—but that does not negate the fact that they most likely got their initial start with the help of a relative or a close friend in a position of power.

Nepotism often gets a bad rap: people perceive it as being "unfair," which it is. You can complain all you want, nepotism will still exist. How can you benefit from nepotism if you do not have any powerful connections from the jump? Simple. Go meet some. You have two choices: give up or get in the game.

When I was trying to land a job out of college, I had zero connections. ZERO. I had to work my butt off to make them. To give you a little bit more context, during my junior year of my undergraduate, I had stopped playing football and had an excess amount of time. I knew that the next year would fly by and I needed to get all of my ducks in a row before I was thrown into the real world. I also knew I needed to take advantage of that time by working and talking to as many people as I possibly could. At the time, I had four part-time jobs simultaneously:

1. Campus Ambassador for Procter and Gamble (Tuesday and Thursday)
2. Production Assistant (Monday–Thursday nights)
3. Leasing Office Specialist (Monday–Friday)
4. Nike Employee Store (Saturday and Sunday)

Even though I was "busy," I knew I eventually needed to land a full-time position. While in college, I made a point to connect with professionals across all industries to help me gain clarity regarding what I wanted to do once I graduated. I met with commercial brokers, bankers, security guards, hotel employees, residential realtors, commercial brokers, and more. By speaking with professionals across numerous industries, I realized I did not want any of their jobs. I wanted to work at Nike HQ.

These "meetings" I was having I later learned had a name—informational interviews. By talking to so many people, I was able to refine my skills; I soon noticed my informational interviews were getting better and better. Ultimately, I learned not only how to ask specific questions, I learned how to add value.

After honing in on my goal to get a job at Nike corporate, I made a point to go on informational interviews during my hour lunch break while working at the Nike employee store (retail). I would schedule each meeting for fifteen minutes. I had my agenda set. A typical lunch break for me meant I'd go to my car and change into business attire. After changing, I'd drive three miles from Nike's employee store to Nike's corporate campus. I would have my meetings in the most high-traffic areas. After the informational interview was over, I'd drive back to the Nike employee store, eat something, and get back to work. I was dialed in. I made an agreement with myself that setting up these meetings for my future self was non-negotiable. I say all this to say, regardless of your current circumstances or how "busy" you are, you can always make time for something that is important to you.

I've since realized that numerous other successful people also went out of their way to incorporate informational interviews into their lives, whether they realized they were doing it or not. Their established connections catapulted their success in their respective fields. Striking up a conversation is one thing, mastering the art of an informational interview is another.

For example, the founder of Front Office Sports, Adam White, had numerous informational interviews prior to launching his career. Initially, he held informational interviews to network with the ultimate goal of getting a job after graduating. While having these interviews, he realized there was an opportunity to showcase stories surrounding the business of the sports industry. Landing a job was no longer Adam's objective, starting his own business was. By having these informational interviews, Adam was able to identify a gap in the market and recognized there was an opportunity for him to create the foundation for his digital editorial company. According to *Bloomberg*, the company is now valued at $25 million. Talk about the power of informational interviews.

In graduate school, learning how to conduct informational interviews was one of my primary focal points. Although I already knew their importance and had implemented them prior to attending graduate school, I was shocked at the sheer number of students who were not yet aware of the power of informational interviews. I can spare you a significant amount of tuition money with the strategies in this book.

Informational interviews can ultimately help you discover more about yourself. By learning about other people's journeys, you will be able to realize how to create the life that you want. You may discover that what you initially thought you wanted is not as appealing as what you once believed. You may also find a faster route to accomplish career goals through other people's mistakes or successes. Informational interviews will ultimately lead to more connections, life-changing epiphanies, and opportunities.

Informational interviews not only landed me a job at Nike HQ, but by continuing to have them throughout my career, they've led me to my true purpose. Informational interviews gave me the courage to pivot when I had doubts. Now as an NFLPA agent and the co-founder of Disruptive Sports Agency, I continue to have informational interviews to make new connections, create more opportunities for my clients, and scale my business.

People often assume I woke up one day, got certified, launched my company, and instantly started signing professional athletes. If it were only that easy! People see the flash, they see the highlights, and they think everything I've accomplished was done overnight. Similar to an NFL star that's featured on ESPN, the average person can see a ten-second clip and think the athlete was blessed with pure talent and that the game just came naturally to them. What the average person doesn't take into account is that, even with natural abilities, the typical professional athlete dedicates their entire life to working on their craft to *potentially* get an opportunity to showcase their skills in the league. There are no handouts. Not in the NFL, not as a sports agent, not as a business owner, not ever.

In theory, conducting informational interviews may sound relatively straightforward. However, it can be quite complex. Upon completion of this book, you will without a doubt be fully equipped to have intentional informational interviews that will knock down barriers to get you on the fast track to your desired destination.

Apply It

If you think you have had informational interviews in the past, list them below.

_____

_____

_____

_____

_____

_____

When were the informational interviews?

_____

_____

_____

_____

_____

Who did you meet?

_____

_____

_____

_____

_____

_____

What was discussed?

_____

_____

_____

_____

_____

_____

How can having more informational interviews advance your desired career or help your business get to the next level?

_____

_____

_____

_____

_____

_____

With what you know now, how can informational interviews save you time?

_____

_____

_____

_____

_____

Chapter 2

Clarity First

"Heroes get remembered but legends never
die. Follow your heart kid, and you'll
never go wrong."
The Babe, The Sandlot

Although you may be fired up to get into the tactical strategies of mastering the informational interview, you must take a moment to get crystal clear about what we are pursuing and why we are pursuing it. In this chapter, I have parsed out strategies for newbies to the workforce, people who are established in their professional career but want to pivot, and freelancers or business owners. Feel free to read the section that applies to you or the whole chapter in its entirety—you never know what you might gain!

Newcomers

Before you throw yourself into the workforce for the first time, it's important to have a general idea of what you want to do for a living. When I say "what you want to do for a living," do not misconstrue that phrase as meaning "what you want to do for the rest of your life." As your career develops, you may find yourself growing in your industry or shifting gears completely later on. Do not get fixated on what you want to do "forever." Rather think about what you want to do now.

There is a huge misconception that what you learned in school or what your parents want you to do is what you must do. If you were looking for a sign or a permission slip to break the rules, here it is. Although they may mean well, stop listening to every single thing someone says.

If you were to remove outsiders' opinions completely, what would you want to do? What comes naturally to you? What do you enjoy doing? Everyone is born with natural gifts. What are yours? If you're saying to yourself, "I'm not good at anything," try harder. There's something you truly love to do. Don't worry about the money. The money will come. If the hours seem to fly by when you're in your flow, that is probably a strong indicator that you're operating in the realm of your purpose. When you're that enthralled with what you're doing, work is enjoyable. If you're constantly checking the clock every second to see if you're closer to being done, it's probably a strong indicator that maybe whatever you're doing is not a fit for you.

You may endure some hardships while trying to launch your career, but your passion should outweigh the roadblocks. There will always be others interested in the position you're interested in. There will be people who want to launch their career with the same company you do.

Taking a deeper dive into figuring out what you want to do requires introspection. Figure out what you're good at. You can't just say you're good at talking to people, because most people are terrible at talking to people. Most of you are not personable and you do not have many connections. Social skills are getting weaker due to how much time most of us are spending on our cell phones. People do not want to hear chipper, surface-level shit. "Yeah, I have personality and I'm a people person." Cool. Why don't you have a job then? Be real with yourself. Take inventory objectively.

Pro Tip

Revisit this chapter at various points throughout your career. As you evolve, so do your personal needs!

I like to apply what I call "The Funnel Concept" to narrow down what I want to do. Let's say I want to work at Nike. The top of the funnel is Nike. The bottom of the funnel is the position and category that I want to go after. They are very specific. You want to weed out the shit you do not want to do.

For example, I knew I wanted to work at Nike, but I didn't really know specifically what I wanted to do. I just knew I wanted to work there; it seemed cool. Using the process of

Pro Tip

Reverse engineer your dates and gates to accomplish your goals.

By setting dates and gates, you will be more prepared. The more prepared you are, the luckier you get. Whenever I met someone, I had a one-page snapshot of my experience along with the projects I was currently working on. I updated it monthly. From this, everyone I met with was able to gather who I was in a nutshell and tell me what my next steps should be. This helped me continue to fine tune my dates and gates.

As a newcomer, you have nothing to lose but everything to gain. To summarize, filter what you want to do, set dates and gates, and be willing to put in the hard work!

elimination, I started to narrow the funnel down. I knew I did not want to work at the front desk. I did not want to work in logistics. I did not want to work in operations or HR. So those were out. I wanted to either work in sales, marketing, or product. I narrowed down what I wanted to do based on the people I met with, who I liked, who I thought I was, and my natural strengths. I eventually ended up narrowing it down to either product or marketing. I fell in love with marketing. You can narrow it down faster by meeting with more people.

As you start informational interviews, understand the company and have an idea of what you want to do. A lot of people go to their dream company and say, "I'll do anything to work here." You can't do that. You have to have a road map or a vision of where you're trying to go. Nobody can point you in the right direction if you don't know where you are going. You increase your chances of getting to that destination if you can figure out what the specific roles are—when they are hiring for those roles, you've already met with a person who can put in a good word for you. The person you met with will potentially reach out to you and tell you about that job opening because it will come up within the internal pages before it ever hits an online job board. Having informational interviews with the right people will keep you top of mind.

If you get offered an internship initially, be okay with it. The best thing somebody can do is not pay you because you learn how to make money yourself. With every employer that did not pay me, I made a ton of connections that provided me with monetary gain in the long term. Especially in the beginning of your career, it is important to know that you are not above anything. You should view everything as an opportunity. Just because you went to a fancy university doesn't mean you will be guaranteed a job or even a paid internship.

I get calls all the time from people in undergrad or grad school inquiring about getting into the sports industry. Recently, I offered a college student an internship and his response to me was, "I'm twenty-seven. I'm too old to intern for free. I have bills to pay." I didn't acknowledge his statement. I instantly knew he didn't have what it takes. He wasn't hungry enough. When I was twenty-eight I had already had multiple salaried roles, but I ultimately realized

I needed to reposition myself in order to become a sports agent. While this decision was not easy by any means, I knew it was my best option. I willingly worked for free in exchange for gaining knowledge. Yes, it was hard, but I grew from the experience and received invaluable information.

I will never understand wanting to be like someone but being unwilling to make sacrifices. When something becomes unfathomable, to me you simply don't want it enough. That old proverb, "where there's a will, there's a way," still rings true. If you have to make a short-term sacrifice for long-term success, why wouldn't you do it? Even if it's "hard," you can always make a plan.

Let's say you have a job but you want to take on an unpaid internship in your desired field. Maybe it's a matter of saying to yourself, "Look I'm in this job, I'm working right now. I'm going to save up X amount of money so I'm able to work for three months for free." When you make that sacrifice, you will maximize your internship. By having an aggressive timeline and holding yourself accountable, you will succeed.

To help create manageable timelines, I like to set what I call dates and gates. Anything can be accomplished with dates and gates. I set dates for goals and certain things have to happen by those dates. It's weird how things have always worked out. At Nike, I said a year to this date I'm not going to be at this job. As I got closer to the year mark, I got hungrier. Dates and gates create checkpoints. For example, at one point I said, "I'm going to be an agent by X date." "I'm going to take my qualifying exam on X." "I'm going to find out I passed on X." "I'm going to sign these clients on X."

Career Swappers

Maybe you've been working in an industry for a while now and you are simply unfulfilled. You're looking to make a change to live a more fulfilled life. You find yourself almost in a daze every day, skating through life just trying to pay the bills. Deep down inside you know you were destined for more.

You want to pivot but you're afraid of the repercussions. When thinking of making a move to another company or another industry altogether you may be asking yourself some or all of the following questions:

- What will my family think if I quit my job?
- What will my current employer think if I leave the company hanging?
- What if I end up not liking or failing at what I decide to do next?
- Why can't I just appreciate where I'm at? If I just stay a little longer, I may be able to be happy further down the line.

If you're constantly asking yourself these questions, it's simply time to make a move. You clearly are having these thought patterns for a reason! If you were truly fulfilled doing what you were doing you wouldn't be asking yourself these questions in the first place. Be real with yourself: you are not happy with your current situation. Are you going to continue to suffer in silence in order to please other people? If you were to continue on the path you're currently on for the next five years, would you be happy or depressed as fuck?

I've had to accept change quite a few times throughout my professional career. I thought I wanted to work solely in marketing for so long. However, the longer I was in the industry and the more people I talked to, I realized that being a sports agent was my true calling. I wanted to make a true impact in my clients' lives and in underserved communities. Letting go of a steady W-2 job that was supposed to provide "security" was actually the one thing that was hindering me from living in my purpose. I had close friends, even family members, trying to discourage me from making certain changes—but I had to make a decision to ignore the noise. Staying clear and focused on my overall objective helped. Having the courage to stick with my gut instinct was one of the best things I could've done.

All this to say, you are not indebted to a job, an industry, or other people's expectations of what you *should* be. Oftentimes, people lose sight of the fact that their life is in their own hands. You are free to pivot at any point in life. Pivoting is hard. Change is never easy. However, the satisfaction of being able to look in the mirror and be content with yourself will always outweigh regret in the end.

If you're serious about making a true change in your life, informational interviews can help you get to where you want to go. You may even eventually ask yourself what took you so long! Sometimes you have to let other people down in order to gain what you truly want. What you say about you will always be more important than what everyone else says about you. Remember that.

Corporate Ladder Climber

Are you already happy in your job or industry and want to climb the corporate ladder faster? You can use informational interviews to your advantage. By having informational interviews with higher-ups in your company or with people in your industry who work for other companies, you can gain a great deal of insight to expedite your growth. Not only can you find out what it takes to have a higher-level position, you can ask questions to figure out if that role is really something you want to take on or if it just sounds better in theory.

The more people you talk to in your ideal role, the more you will discover if there's work-life balance in that role, what those people like and dislike about it—in short, you will get answers that tons of people do not get until they are actually in that role. Having informational interviews with people who are living out your future life will also make the role seem more obtainable in a shorter time frame.

You should always make informational interviews a habit, even when you land your ideal role. A lot of people stop networking once they get the job they want. People get so fixated on wanting to be the best at their current role, they forget to have a backup plan. The reality is, you can get fired from any job at any given time with limited or no notice. A new term for creating this safety net is called "career cushioning." Essentially, career cushioning means you're creating a plan B without actively trying to land a new job. We have seen massive Big Tech layoffs in 2022 and 2023, and will surely continue to, regardless of the year—job security can change on a dime. No one is immune to layoffs or unforeseen circumstances. Witnessing others go through an unpredictable job market should serve as a reminder to never stop updating your résumé or establishing more connections, regardless of your current job status.

Entrepreneurs

Informational interviews are for entrepreneurs at any level. Whether you are a solopreneur, a small-business owner, or have a massive company, informational interviews should play an essential role in your business. Taking your business to the next level will always require you to meet more people to gain more knowledge, consider different perspectives, and look for new opportunities.

As an entrepreneur myself, I know that sometimes we take on the "can-do" attitude to the point that it can even become detrimental to our business. Being an entrepreneur, at some point you've probably served as the accountant, the marketing guru, the copywriter, the salesman, the CEO, and much more. You may have a team and may have delegated certain tasks at this point in your career. However, you MUST go outside of your own company in order to level it up.

We do ourselves an injustice when we think we have all the answers. Having informational interviews can serve you and your company in more ways than you might think. You may be able to scale faster, gain a fresh perspective, or simply build up your network. I make a point to schedule at least two informational interviews a month. I was also able to purchase my first home and close on two different investment properties shortly after completing undergrad by talking to the right people while still in school. I had a goal of generating passive income before completion of grad school. Since I focused heavily on making the right connections, I was able to reach that goal with all the information I had acquired. Being an entrepreneur can get hectic, but informational interviews should be built into your schedule.

As you know, starting and sustaining a business for the long-term is no easy feat. In fact, data from the US Bureau of Labor Statistics shows that approximately 20 percent of new businesses fail during the first two years of being open, 45 percent during the first five years, and 65 percent during the first ten years. Only 25 percent of new businesses make it to fifteen years or more.[*] The statistics haven't fluctuated much over time and have been relatively consistent since the 1990s. I do not mention this to scare you or be a Debbie

---

[*]   https://www.bls.gov/bdm/us_age_naics_00_table7.txt
Article that dissected the data: https://www.investopedia.com/financial-edge/1010/top-6-reasons-new-businesses-fail.aspx

Downer. I say this to remind you that as an entrepreneur, you must continuously strive to be inquisitive not only for yourself, but for your business.

A huge reason why my company has had some early success is due to the fact that informational interviews have enabled me to obtain more deals, to hire for key roles within the company, and to keep me up to date on a rapidly changing industry. The key is as an entrepreneur to not only work in the business, but on the business. Informational interviews help broaden your scope to blind spots you may have.

Newcomer

If a dollar sign was not attached to your work, what are a few things you're passionate about? Write about why you're drawn to those things. By doing this you will begin creating your funnel.

_____

_____

_____

_____

_____

_____

_____

_____

_____

_____

_____

_____

_____

_____

_____

_____

_____

_____

_____

_____

_____

_____

_____

Career Swapper

Write a personal note to yourself about how you will feel in your current role/venture for another five years. Write another short personal note to yourself about how you'd feel pursuing something you're passionate about in the next five years. In both scenarios, what are the pros and cons?

_____

_____

_____

_____

_____

_____

_____

_____

_____

_____

_____

_____

_____

_____

_____

_____

_____

_____

_____

_____

Corporate Ladder Climber

What have you done thus far to elevate in your field? What do you do exceptionally well in your current role? What habits may be holding you back? Be honest.

_____

_____

_____

_____

_____

_____

_____

_____

_____

_____

_____

_____

_____

_____

_____

_____

_____

_____

_____

_____

_____

_____

_____

_____

Entrepreneur

Take inventory of the last quarter in your business. What items in your company's control need improvement? How do these current weaknesses affect your business? Can you think of anyone else or a company that can help improve this weak area within your company?

Chapter 3

Inward for Onward

"The people who are crazy enough to think
they can change the world are the ones
who do."
Steve Jobs

Before we get into the nitty gritty, you need to remember—no matter what goal you are chasing—the importance of truly being in tune with yourself. If you stay true to who you are, you will always be on the right track. The phrase "authentic self" gets thrown around so much these days, sometimes we forget the true meaning of it. Being your authentic self means staying true to who you are at your deepest core. Your authentic self is your true character before the world told you who, what, why, and how you needed to be.

Once the world piles it's expectations on us, we

oftentimes wake up as a fragmented version of who we truly are. So much so in fact that if you do not work to stay in tune with your authentic self, you can feel like you're having an out-of-body experience, living a life to appease others instead of checking in with yourself first. Once you're able to look inward from an honest place, you will be able to answer the majority of your toughest personal questions. When there's too much outside chatter or mixed messages from various sources, your authentic self can get convoluted in the whirlwind of fleeting opinions. For this reason, I'm a huge proponent of mediation.

Meditation is a tool to drown out whatever is going on externally, and to give you the solace required to dig deep within yourself. I used to think meditation was too "woo woo"—until I realized I had no access to my inner guide without it. Trust me, I know it is not easy to start meditating. I had the attention span of a squirrel when I first started. As someone with diagnosed ADHD, I can tell you it does get easier to settle into the meditation with time. Once you are able to quiet the chatter, your own inner voice can serve as a compass, guiding you in the right direction.

Self-discovery will beget the ultimate confidence in whatever journey you do decide to embark on. When you truly know yourself, you will know without a shadow of a doubt what your passion is, what your true character is, and what you are capable of. Sure, it is going to take work to reach your final destination, but truly knowing who you are and what you are made of will dismantle the trivial mental barriers that may arise, trying to dissuade you from pursuing your ultimate purpose.

Iconic Predecessors

Sometimes your predecessors will leave clues, helping you remember who you are. Sometimes you will come across them in your lifetime; sometimes they're so embedded in you that although you may have never met them in the flesh, their ancestral voices will be powerful enough to reach you in ways that may be unexplainable.

For me, I was fortunate to have two powerful predecessors. Those predecessors, who make it easier to decipher the complexity of my authentic self, were and remain my two late grandfathers. Although I wish I could have spent more time with both of them, I'm still able to learn from each of them, even without them being here physically. Knowing we had the same blood running through our veins gives me unshakeable confidence, even when doubt arises.

Ed Devine: The Man with the Plan

On my mom's side, my Grandpa William Devine ("Ed") serves as a reminder not only of where I come from, but of who I am. My Grandpa Ed went to Cal Poly San Louis Obispo, and became one of the first black engineers at IBM. He eventually went to Hawaii to be a part of their think tank. When he got there, he was instantly intrigued by IBM's marketing and sales people. He loved how sharp they were. From how they inspired others to how they presented themselves—always dressing to the nines. Specifically, he loved their blue suits. Later, he decided to transition to sales and marketing. While he refined many skills during his tenure at IBM, he also never stopped checking in with himself. IBM offered him a big promotion during a time when a black man getting a promotion (or even a job) at IBM was simply unheard of. After much contemplation, he decided to turn the promotion down. His rationale was if they were going to pay him that much to simply think in Hawaii, why not just think for himself?

When he decided to think for himself, he wasn't sure what exactly he wanted to do, but he did know that he wanted to work for himself. Grandpa Ed told me, "I could cook, but I did not want to be a chef. They work all day and your success is dependent upon if others deem your food as being good. I was also a hell of a gardener, but I didn't want to be a landscaper either. I wanted to make money around the clock without arduous labor. I wanted to make money while I was sleeping. The only way to make money when I was sleeping was to buy real estate and get people to pay me money to live in my place."

Grandpa Ed's first real estate deal was in Austin, Texas. A woman had three different properties that Grandpa wanted to buy. Initially, he did not have the funds to purchase all three properties. With creativity, he was able to start his real estate portfolio after the seller agreed to let him purchase all three properties by utilizing a seller carry. With sheer confidence in himself and a will to make his dreams come to fruition he catapulted his career as a real estate investor. He followed up that initial real estate deal with another home he built from the ground up in Texas. He was truly a visionary; the blueprints he had drawn up would be considered modern even to this day.

Eventually, Grandpa Ed made his way to California and built his own version of a real estate empire. He owned all of Havenscourt in Oakland, California. With limited mentorship, he got into a few bad loans with loan sharks. The predatory lenders ran the tab up on him. But even though he got himself into some financial trouble early on in his endeavors, he taught his sons well. Eventually his sons, Eric and Greg Devine, took over the business and short-sold the properties to get out of the bad deals they were in. Eric and Greg bought bigger buildings that were more profitable. They were able to take what their dad taught them and take it to the next level by implementing technology to run numbers more efficiently and accurately in comparison to what their dad was able to do on a ledger.

From Grandpa Ed I learned not only a plethora of life lessons, but I learned what I was made of.

Grandpa Ed's 5 Principles:

1. It all starts with a vision.
2. Never listen to anyone who hasn't been to where you want to go. If you can get the vision in your mind, you can do it.

3. Find the man that's done what you want to do successfully and listen to him.

4. Don't be late. Ever. Cuz' when you're late you lose and when you lose it's nobody's fault but your own. (Though I might add he considered on time late. Be early. I learned that lesson with him the hard way.)

Don't be about the bullshit. Hold yourself accountable. Be real with yourself when you're winning AND losing.

Dr. Claude Organ: The Legendary Surgeon

On my dad's side, my other iconic predecessor is my Grandpa Dr. Claude Organ, who I refer to as "Papa." Papa was from Denison, Texas. He received his education in the segregated schools of Denison along with his two siblings. Despite his circumstances, he was the valedictorian at Terrell High School. Papa's parents instilled in him a strong sense of dignity and self-worth that did not allow them to think of themselves as less than their counterparts. Papa had to take a bold approach to get into medical school after graduating from Xavier University. With his relentless persistence he was accepted into Creighton University's medical school, as they were the first Roman Catholic Medical School to integrate their student body.

Papa left a legacy. After finishing his residency and fulfilling his service commitment in Camp Pendleton, he came back to Creighton and began an academic surgical career

that spanned forty-five years. From 1960–1982 he advanced
through the academic ranks. The last eleven years, Papa was
the Chief of the Department of Surgery, creating a wildly
sought-after general surgery
residency training program.
During his time in Omaha,
Nebraska, Papa and Warren
Buffett met through the Urban
League, before the world knew
who Warren Buffett was. After
the two got to know each
other, Warren Buffett became
Papa's client and dear friend.

In the early days of Warren
Buffett's investing, he asked Papa to give him $100,000 to
invest. The catch: Buffett told Papa he would not be able
to touch the money for at least ten years. Although Papa
knew Buffet was sharp even without a proven track record,
he didn't have $100,000 to give at the time. Papa had a total
of seven kids. Since he valued education, he was using all
of his funds to put them through college. Those colleges
included Stanford, Southern Methodist, and Harvard. Papa's
ultimate goal was to pull his entire family out of poverty in
one generation. Even though he didn't have the $100,000 to
give to Buffett at the time, Papa knew he could later utilize
him somehow, someway. Down the line Papa was the only
black man on the Boys Town board, later helping Warren
Buffet get on the Boys Town board as well. However, Papa

> **Pro Tip**
> When we begin asking multiple people the same question, oftentimes we are just searching for validation, not necessarily an answer. The question is, when are you going to start validating yourself?

wasn't made a billionaire by Buffet like the other doctors who invested with him early on.

From 1982–1988, Papa was a professor at the University of Oklahoma and Chief of Surgery at the Veterans Administration Hospital. In 1988, he took on a surgery residency program in surgical service at Highland Hospital in Oakland, California. Once again Papa built up the faculty and developed the residency into another widely sought-after training program. Papa served as the second black president of the American College of Surgeons.

With all that Papa accomplished in his life, his persistent pursuit of growth is what still resonates with me to this day.

Dr. Claude Organ's Principles:
1.   Education is key.
2.   What's in your head no one can take away from you, except you.
3.   A routine is crucial in fulfilling long-term goals.
4.   Once you're let in the door and you learn the rules, you have two more responsibilities—to be excellent in everything you do and to show others the way.

Quote lived by: "Destiny is not a matter of chance. It is a matter of choice. It is not a thing to be waited for; it is a thing to be achieved." — William Jennings Bryan

Although looking within yourself for answers may seem difficult to achieve at first, the more you try to discover who you are at your core, the easier decision-making will become.

If an opportunity agrees with who you are, you'll know; and if it is against what you stand for, you'll know that as well.

Principles

Based on your findings in the Apply It section on pages 22-23, create a list of principles to live by. The principles should be congruent with your authentic self. Not who you wish to be, but who you are.

Chapter 4

Set Lofty Goals

"Shoot for the moon and you will land
amongst the stars."
Les Brown

So you're beginning to do the inner work to take steps
in the right direction for you. What's next? Prior to
setting up informational interviews, you need to set lofty
goals. Think big. When's the last time you set a massive goal?
When I say lofty goal, I am not talking about something that
can be achieved overnight. A lofty goal should take you an
extended period of time in order to accomplish it.

Generally, we think setting the bar low will help us feel
better. Why? We are simply afraid we will never succeed
if we set it too high. If we don't succeed, we get into our
heads and go down the fear rabbit hole. We start to doubt

ourselves before we even try. Setting the bar low gives us a way to accomplish rudimentary goals; we set easily achievable goals to provide us with a sure ego boost. We naturally want to create a safe haven in our minds to completely eliminate the possibility of having to face all of the "what if" scenarios if we fall on our ass.

I got comfortable setting lofty goals in the beginning of my professional career. When I was working at the Nike retail store, I knew that was just a starting point for me to eventually work in Nike HQ. I told myself I was not going to be in the retail store for more than one year. I already had my two weeks resignation notice signed and on auto-pilot to send out. I chose to work at the Nike retail store part-time. I was not going to be caught up working there full-time—not to knock it, but I knew I had to set unrealistic expectations to get where I was trying to go.

When I was at the Nike employee store I had a group of three people (we called ourselves the Triangle) who were trying to get out of there. We'd practice and talk about how informational interviews went. We'd share information about people we met, and those stories would help us know more people even if we didn't personally meet them. We knew about them, knew what they did, so we were able to develop the pieces of the workflow and solve a few questions that we had. On your journey to doing things that no one in your circle has done, going at it alone makes it so much harder. I did not yet know that there was a process to meeting people. You gotta find like-minded individuals who are your age and are trying to do what you're trying to do. If they don't exist, then you have to make a group.

I reached my goal before the others. Although they eventually all made it out of retail, I was able to leave the retail store sooner because they were more hyper-focused on making money. They worked too many hours at the Nike employee store when I could do twenty hours at the store but also spend twenty hours on the Nike campus. They would only get to spend five hours a week on the campus, so I got to my goal way faster than them.

People always say money isn't everything. Yes, money is everything. I've heard people who do not value money say that money isn't everything and yet they work for it like slaves and peasants. You have to make strategic investments in yourself in order to get into your next phase. In order for me to get to the Nike campus making $50,000 a year, I had to work less at the employee store and make less money so I could spend more time investing in myself to get there.

They said they had to have the money. I sacrificed money in the short term to reach my destination faster. When I looked at the numbers, instead of making $25,000 working full-time at the Nike employee store, I made a choice to play the long game. I only made $10,000—but the following year I made $50,000. $10,000 + $50,000 = $60,000. On the other hand, my counterparts worked at the employee store and only made $50,0000 over the course of those two years. Slow and steady does not always win the race.

How can you do this and stay afloat? You must get creative. I had three part-time jobs. I worked at my apartment complex on the weekdays to pay my rent. On the weekends, I worked at the Nike employee store. I also worked for a production company at night during the week. I ended up making $25k the first year with more jobs and more exposure.

Once I stopped playing football I had way too much spare time. I was trying to make something out of myself. I wasn't always the most talented or most gifted but I just loved work. It was fun. I love making money. I've always loved making money, but it always comes with a sacrifice.

Even after I was able to break out of the Nike retail store and landed the job at Nike HQ as a Nike Football Brand Marketing Specialist, I never stopped setting new goals. I always ask myself, "What's next?"

After two years in my Nike corporate role, I wanted to become a Nike Ekin. *Ekin* is Nike spelled backwards. An Ekin is a brand ambassador and a go-to person in a given area who pushes the Nike brand. You're an influencer. Everyone who gets to be an Ekin gets an Ekin tattoo on their leg. It's like a fraternity and is considered to be the graduate school of Nike. You have to be special to be an Ekin.

I wanted to be an Ekin at the time because I thought it would complement my attributes and would help me get back to my family in the Bay Area. San Francisco was going to be my area, so I thought.

I did two years of free volunteer work to prepare. I did multiple shoe activations, built pitch decks, drove from

"Hood to Coast" (a twenty-four-hour Nike race), did consumer insight projects, consumer tested shoes, did grunt tasks to make my potential boss's life easier. All to become top of mind when a job in the category became available. When a position did open, I shot a recap video and flew to New York for the interview. I did all this shit. I ultimately did not get the job. They said I was "overqualified." It was a lower-bandwidth job. Even though they knew that was my territory, leadership thought it would impede my success. When I didn't get the job, I realized I did not want to go for a bigger corporate role in Nike HQ. I needed to set the bar higher.

Pro Tip

Go out there and get it. Shoot for the moon so you can land amongst the stars. If a UFO lands on your front porch, you get in. You do not ask questions; you get in. If a great opportunity lands in front of your face, you figure it out. You don't say what you can't do or what you're gonna do. You just figure it the fuck out.

So after not getting the Ekin job, I knew it was time to leave. I put in my two weeks notice. Sometimes when you're kicked down, you begin to try to make sense of everything. Upon deeper reflection, I knew I was a natural-born entrepreneur. I've always had an entrepreneurial spirit. Thinking back, I tried to remember what truly brought me joy. The truth is, I found joy in making deals happen. In elementary school I had numerous business ventures:

1. I started out selling cologne in first grade. I would take cologne samples, mix it with water and Mentos in a water bottle, and sell it to everyone at school.
2. A teacher also saw me cleaning shoes once and he asked me to shine his. I charged him $5 and made sure they were spick and span when I gave them back. I did such a good job, more teachers started inquiring.
3. I would collect coins, but instead of going to Coin-star, I would avoid the 10 percent surcharge and go to the bank to roll the coins and get the full amount.
4. I would buy "exclusive" shoes and clothes at the mall and resell them.
5. I would have my mom buy snacks and drinks in bulk and charge other students a premium during recess and lunch.

Being an entrepreneur wasn't something I simply wanted to do, I knew it was always within me, I just needed to bet on myself.

After my time in corporate, I created a modeling agency that helped my friends land modeling gigs at Nike. I was constantly looking for models that were also athletes. Since I had a wide range of athletic friends, my first entrepreneurial venture thrived. I was helping my friends tremendously and paid them handsomely, sometimes $1,000 a day. During this time, I also helped someone I consider one of my mentors today—attorney Adam G. Snyder—rebrand his sports agency. I not only learned the inner workings of the sports agency world, I learned how to run a business.

Sometimes it takes other people to recognize and remind you of your personal strengths in order for you to create your next lofty goal. In my case, I did not actually want to be a sports agent. I had friends who kept telling me to become one. One of my childhood best friends, Najee Lovett, was one of the first to tell me he thought I should become an agent. Najee was a stellar collegiate football player who honestly could've made it to the league if he would've had the right representation at the time. When I was running my modeling business, Najee told me, "You really have the ability to hype players up if you believe in someone. It's not like you're lying, you're telling the truth. You have a ton of confidence in your delivery and in turn it makes the player that much more confident."

Razor, another friend, happened to say something similar out of the blue around the same time. Razor invited me to breakfast. I genuinely thought he wanted to meet so I could join some multi-level marketing bullshit that he was part of. To my surprise, he motivated me to become an agent. Razor sat me down and explained, "Henry, you can really easily convey a message to people and they trust you based on what you say and how you word things. The way you're authentic and at the same time a complete fucking asshole, you need to be an agent. There are people out here that will pay you to become an agent, you are that good." Both Najee and Razor saw something in me that I did not fully see in myself.

I then took another leap of faith and set the lofty goal of going back to school to obtain my master's degree in order to become a sports agent. I wanted to graduate early and get licensed as soon as possible. Simultaneously, I got a job at Equinox as a sales manager in order to generate some income while I was going to school full-time. I set another huge goal to make as much money as possible in that role. I dominated. I was breaking sales records and averaging $16,000 a month.

It just so happened that the sports agency internship I had inquired about right before attending graduate school (with one of the biggest agencies on the West Coast) finally got back to me and wanted me to start. The problem was, I was now settled into this job and the internship was unpaid. I ran the calculations and I weighed my opportunity costs. I had two options: I could play it safe and do it the direct route (keep the job, graduate, and make my way to a sports agency later) or be aggressive (quit the job, learn as much as possible at the internship, and figure the rest out). I figured this opportunity with a major sports agency wouldn't come around often, so I took the risk. I left the job and agreed to the internship.

When I got to the internship, I felt like I had made a huge mistake. I was spending money just to get to the internship and had zero cash flow. But despite all the drawbacks, I learned how to become an agent at an accelerated rate. From this one experience as an intern, I learned I could become an agent even faster than what I had initially thought. Instead of waiting to graduate with my secondary degree, I could apply to take the NFLPA agent exam because I had enough contract negotiation experience from my previous jobs under my belt. Had I not decided to take the leap of faith with the unpaid internship, I wouldn't be an agent and there would be no Disruptive. The following year COVID happened and the NFLPA agent exam was cancelled. If I had not taken my test that year (or failed) it would have delayed my plans for two years.

While I was at the renowned sports agency, I not only realized that I wanted to become certified, I realized that I needed to build my own agency—not join one. This wasn't a money grab for me; I genuinely wanted to pursue the best interest of each and every client I represented and set them up for success. I realized many of the established agencies told players what they wanted to hear, had the players sign, and once the agent got their commission they were on to the next biggest upcoming athlete and failed to uphold their end of the bargain when it came down to taking care of the players. I wanted to operate differently. I wanted the players to build generational wealth and be able to positively impact their community, even when their playing days were over.

Although a tedious undertaking, I knew it was my bigger purpose. In order to operate how I wanted to as an agent, I knew I had to make my own vision come to life. I not only passed the NFLPA agency exam, I secured funding for Disruptive, signed clients I felt aligned with my overall vision

I had for the company, and began to foster solid business relationships. You have to be intentional, draw inspiration from others, and have the confidence to act on your plans.

Setting Unrealistic Goals for Your Dreams

To this day, I still set lofty goals. When I tell people how I want to disrupt the entire sports agency industry, many people think I'm crazy. You know what's crazy to me? Not even trying to reach your full potential. What's even crazier is that people will try to delegitimize your dreams, just because they do not have the courage to live out theirs. For this reason, when you set your lofty goals, it's crucial to only share them with like-minded people who will encourage you to think even bigger.

You have to realize that everything on this earth that we see today was made up by people who were really not that intelligent. You have to dream about who you want to be and work backwards to figure it out. Only once you've begun working toward those dreams should you lower expectations based on what you can and cannot do. If you are unable to think big, this book is probably a waste of your time, so go ahead and give it to somebody else.

We are going to get morbid for a minute, so buckle up. If we look at the cold hard facts of your future, one thing is for sure—you will be on your deathbed one day. I want you to imagine your final moments, you start thinking about all the things you never did. All the things you "coulda, woulda, shoulda" did. What legacy will you leave behind? What will you have to do now to leave that legacy behind?

Legacy

Write your own obituary. What do other people say about your character? What are your biggest accomplishments? What people did you help? How was the world left a better place?

_____

_____

_____

_____

_____

_____

_____

_____

_____

_____

_____

_____

_____

_____

_____

_____

_____

_____

_____

_____

Chapter 5

The Board

"It is important to surround yourself with
people who lift you up, encourage you,
share your vision, and inspire you."
Les Brown

Before you jump into attempting to land informational interviews, it's vital to have the right people in your corner to keep you on the right track. I refer to these integral people as "The Board."

In business, a board of directors is a governing body that is responsible for protecting shareholders' interests, establishing various policies, having complete oversight, and making decisions regarding vital issues a company may face. Sounds important, right? It is. It's crucial.

You too need your own board of directors. Your board

of directors are specific mentors you need in your life, all with their own unique perspective. Throughout your life the board will change. People leave the board, people drop out of the board, and as you go on, your board can look tremendously different depending on where you're at in life. Though the people change, the positions remain the same. These mentors will help you get in front of more people— but more importantly, the right people. Since your mentors will most likely be well connected, you will have the opportunity to have meaningful informational interviews through their connections. Let's take a closer look into the five board member positions that should be a constant in your life.

The Expert

If you want to be an expert in your field, you must align yourself with someone who already is. Not a rookie, not an average Joe, an expert. The expert has a proven track record. If everything was taken away from the expert, they should firmly believe they could build their empire back up from scratch, or even surpass where they were prior to everything being stripped away by using all of the lessons they have already learned. The expert has ultimate confidence that stems from a place of experience. Since they did it once, they wholeheartedly believe they can do it again.

Do you have a concept you're not sure will succeed? Ask the expert. Want to stay in your industry but maybe switch roles? Ask the expert. Not sure how to continue to evolve in a rapidly changing industry? Ask the expert. Not sure if your boss is an asshole or you're just being soft? Ask the expert.

Since the expert probably will not be able to offer you much time, be sure to be prepared every time you get a chance to talk. When talking to your expert, get to the point, be open-minded, and listen more than you speak. If you'd like help regarding finding a solution to your problem, be sure to explain the issues you're grappling with and your desired outcome in a concise way. Surely your expert has experienced a similar dilemma at some point in their career.

If you have an expert mentor in mind and do not yet know them, get creative in your pursuit of a relationship. Do you have a mutual connection? Can someone you know possibly introduce you? Can you scour the internet to find their email address and send them a brief message?

When people think of expert mentors, they often assume they are "unreachable." When people have achieved a certain level of success in their career (and have received the highest level of praise) people tend to want to see them as a superhero. Get over being intimidated or starstruck by the expert. Remember that the expert is human and was once in the same exact place you are: a newbie. I'm not telling you to build a relationship with an alien that just touched down from outer space—damn! Experts are human! Relax and go find the expert you want to build a relationship with in your field, you'll be surprised who is actually willing to help if you'd just ask.

If the expert in your field is truly unreachable, people

have such an online presence these days it is easy to grab bits and pieces of information directly from your desired expert and apply them to your life. Keep working hard enough and one day the expert you've been keen on connecting with will also want to connect with you.

For me, my expert is Ray Anderson. He has done everything pertaining to football. Ray was Roger Goodell's right-hand man, was the GM of the Atlanta Falcons, and represented most of the head black football coaches in the NFL. Since he has so much experience in his field, he's direct and candid as hell. When I think of someone who has earned their stripes and can speak on myriad topics from personal experience, I think of Ray.

Key Attributes of the Expert
- Industry leader with a proven track record
- Exudes confidence
- Not a fan of sugar-coating, tells it like it is

The Champ

The Champ is here. The champ mentor is *your* champion, a personal advocate for you who will always have your back. If you ever need to list a reference, your champion should always be top of mind. They know how to capture your strengths with their words. If you actually do use them as a reference for anything, they will seal the deal.

The champ mentor doesn't just have your back when

it comes to speaking highly of you, they can also connect you with the right people. The champ mentor has a keen understanding of what makes you tick and what you'd like to accomplish. Since the champ has a solid understanding of who you are and who you'd like to become, they have an internal sense of who from their network would be a good person for you to meet, work related or not.

What's wonderful about the champ is they are able to see the strengths you may not be aware of. By making you aware of your strengths, the champ allows you to refine and improve them. People have a tendency to doubt themselves and think their strengths are commonplace. The champ is your hype man who will make you realize your unique skill sets are powerful and need to be shared with the world.

I am fortunate enough to have two champions: my Uncle Greg and my Uncle Eric. Although they are real estate moguls, they also happen to be my biggest advocates. In business deals, they are strong closers. They help me both personally and professionally without ever asking for any favors. (Side note: You should always provide value back to people, especially the ones who never ask for their help to be reciprocated.)

Key Attributes of the Champ

- Speaks highly of you
- Connects you with people you can benefit from
- Makes you aware of all of your strengths and weaknesses
- Provides a different perspective

The Peer

How can someone who is your peer be your mentor? While it may seem like an oxymoron, your peer mentor is someone you work closely with or who has goals that are similar to yours. The peer is like a co-pilot; they can talk to you about day-to-day situations no one else may be equipped to understand. Seek out a mentor peer who is not only like-minded but isn't afraid of being vulnerable. When someone is driven, they can often feel like they are battling issues on their own. By having a peer in your corner, you are not the only one feeling out the complex situations. You'd be surprised how often your peer will be going through a similar situation almost simultaneously.

Generally, when people are still working to establish themselves, they will put up a facade like things are going better than they actually are. Not to throw anyone under the bus, but some of my own friends sometimes act

Pro Tip

On the days that you accomplish more than usual, take note of what you did and how you were able to accomplish more. Did you get more sleep the night prior? Wake up earlier? On the contrary, when you have an unproductive day, figure out the root cause of your stagnation. Did you get sucked into other people's drama? Were you scrolling on Instagram for five hours? If you get to the root of the problem, you can usually catch how your day went downhill.

like everything is all peaches, when I can look at their faces and know they're going through some shit. Most people want to seem like they have everything figured out to feel more secure or gain approval from others. Knowing this, it is crucial that your mentor peer be someone who prides themselves on being transparent. The more transparent you and your peers are with each other, the faster you will be able to help each other and grow.

I consider Toney Scott my go-to peer mentor. Toney is also an NFLPA-certified agent who just happened to get his certification at the same time as I did. We call each other a few times a week to check in and discuss NFL updates, share industry-specific information, and keep each other in the know.

In regards to the peer, you do not need to be similar in skillset, but you should be similar in drive. Both should be equally yoked when it comes to your desire to get better. With this particular relationship, you should both benefit from having each other around. You and your peer mentor should feel comfortable calling each other on your own shit and should both be open to feedback. This isn't to tear each other down but to hold you both to the highest standard, which will enable you both to reach your full potential. You should be collaborating on long-term goals, discussing ways to improve, and benefitting from each other's unique abilities. Peers can seem like competition, but the way to win is by viewing your counterparts as key resources. If you view everyone in the industry you want to be in or are currently in solely as competition, you will be great at accumulating enemies. Get great at acquiring long-term friends who will also one day be powerhouses in their own right.

Key Attributes of the Peer
- On a similar path
- Extremely transparent and vulnerable
- Gives advice but also asks for your input

The Rock

Everybody has somebody they call when shit hits the fan. That's your rock. The rock mentor is solid. The rock is a person who is always there when you need them. Throughout your life you will experience loss, hardship, and the list goes on. Life will always have a ton of unexpected twists and turns. It's part of the game.

The rock does not have to be industry specific; in fact, it could be a family member or a friend. This should be someone you deeply trust and who you are comfortable opening up to. "Opening up" in this context doesn't mean surface-level shit like the outfit you should wear to your next meeting or what position you want to have in five years. You should be comfortable telling them your greatest fears, what gives you anxiety, and what's going well or not so well in all facets of your life. You need to be able to go below the surface with this person. My mom, Annette Devine, is my rock. She loves me unconditionally and has always been there for me. Even when she doesn't agree with

Wai Lee (left), owner of M.A.C. computer store in Berkeley, California, with me. It was my first job before going into high school and I was one of Mr. Lee's first hires when he purchased the store.

I have always had a white board and kept a to-do list. This was my office back in the day—in the corner of my first apartment out of college.

My grandfather, Dr. Claude H. Organ. He was an internationally known surgeon and educator and the second African American to serve as president of The American College of Surgeons.

From left to right: My uncle Greg Devine, my grandpa Ed Devine, and my uncle Eric Devine. My grandpa was one of the first Black engineers at IBM. He also was a real estate investor who passed his legacy onto his kids.

From left to right: My uncle Greg, Jerry Beverly, and uncle Eric Devine with me in front of one of the Devine investment properties in Oakland, California.

From left to right: Adam Snyder, Don Williams (of the Super Bowl champion Philadelphia Eagles), and me. Adam was one of the first people to encourage me to become an NFL agent.

The Nike Dunk SB Wet Floor, designed by Ian Williams.

My second investment property, an eight-unit building in Oakland, California.

A commercial for Riddell for their Speedflex helmets in 2015. I supplied the models from my modeling agency, Focus Models. I also was a technical director for the video shoot.

With my Disruptive co-founder, Hector Rivas. Hector was also of Thrift Books.

Me when I first signed Kendrick Bourne at my house with my mom; Kendrick's brothers, Evan Bourne and Andrew Bourne; and their kids.

Kendrick Bourne and me after he got paid by the New England Patriots—a three-year, $22.5 million-dollar deal.

An interview with Matt Maiocco, a beat reporter for the San Francisco 49ers, during Super Bowl LVI in Los Angeles, California.

Brennan Scarlet of The Miami Dolphins and me recording a podcast for B Scar TV.

From left to right: Samori Toure of the Green Bay Packers, me, and Darius Clemons of the University of Michigan.

From left to right: Devin Asiasi of the Cincinnati Bengals, me, and Kendrick Bourne at a Big Brothers Big Sisters Foundation golfing event.

Samori Toure and me before Green Bay played in San Francisco against the 49ers.

From left to right: Trainer Aaron Woods, Kendrick Bourne, and me working out right before free agency.

Picture of me at home preparing right before the draft.

Me speaking to aspiring entrepreneurs regarding the importance of making more connections.

Kendrick Bourne and me two days before he gets paid by the New England Patriots, on our way to donate 100 laptops during the COVID-19 pandemic to kids in Oakland, California.

my decisions, she supports me.

Having a rock mentor will serve as a soundboard for life. The rock will make the twists and turns of your life seem less chaotic. They can help you think clearly when your thoughts get a little hazy. The rock will always be able to put things into perspective for you whether it is work related, family related, or if you just need to vent. Everyone needs a rock.

Key Attributes of the Rock
- Non-judgmental
- Always solution-oriented
- Extremely reliable

The Young Buck

Ah, the young buck mentor. Often misconstrued as too young to know anything, the young buck can be a valuable asset to you regardless of their age. While you might be quite young yourself, it always pays to have someone younger to go to for advice. Usually people think of youngsters solely as mentees. However, I'd like for you to consider the young buck as a mentor too.

The older a person gets, the wiser they become. On the other hand, the young buck tends to be "in the know." Whether it's how to navigate the newest tech app, what's "trending," or how to connect better with the younger demographic.

The youngster gets discredited way too quickly. There's a reason why you've probably heard someone say "you keep me young" a few times throughout your life. Youth should be celebrated. As you get older, you'll realize the young bucks can offer a ton of foresight and have an insane pulse on what's going on across multiple industries.

Also, if you write the young buck off too quickly and do not build any relationships with the youth, you are potentially missing out on big opportunities. As the world continues to evolve at a rapid pace, the young buck could catch a big break and be highly successful. You never know who someone will become. Learn to not discriminate. Treat everyone like you can learn something from them, because you can.

My young buck is Tevin Tavares. Tevin is a prominent young film director. He is the director of *Top Class*, a TV show featuring LeBron James's son, Bronny. Tevin is always around young energy, he's hip. He is young enough to know what his generation and the younger deem as "cool." TikTok trends, the latest dance, etc. He is in the know right now. He's got a lot of swag. Keep a Tevin around to keep you youthful.

Key Attributes of the Young Buck
- Has a pulse on what's trending in the world
- Has superb foresight
- Optimistic about the future

Stay Connected to Your Board

List out all the ways you can continue to stay connected to your board members. There are no bad ideas. Visit this list when you need inspiration to rekindle a relationship.

Part II

The Mastery

Chapter 6

Habits

"Put action to support the intention. Don't say, 'I want to be a millionaire,' but then don't take the activities to do it. Have the vision of what you want to become, but you have to put consistent action behind that vision in order for that to manifest, and it has to be consistent."

Robert F. Smith

In order to put your best foot forward when trying to land informational interviews and make the most of them, your daily habits are paramount to building your version of success. If you have little to no structure, it will be difficult to build positive momentum toward your next goal. Ultimately, positive or negative habits will compound; it is your duty to make sure your habits are compounding in your favor.

Although life will always throw curveballs at each of us, it is crucial to control what we can control as much as possible. Of course, every day won't be perfect, but if you consistently move in the right direction, you will ultimately have more productive days than lackluster ones. I find that when I stick to the same morning and nighttime routines, each and every day I make progress, regardless of what life throws at me.

Establishing a Morning Routine

I wholeheartedly believe that if you win the morning, you win the day. If you create a routine you follow on a daily basis you will be able to set the tone for the rest of the day. I've noticed when I do not follow my routine, I don't feel like I'm fully in control of my day. If I look at my phone when I first wake up and start responding to messages, I instantly become more reactive. By answering to others first and not checking in with yourself, you're at the beck and call of the world rather than operating from a position of power. For this reason, I like to set an intention for the day, feed my mind, and move my body before interacting with others and diving into work. I set an intention in order to recalibrate myself; then I get honest with myself about what I want to focus on for that day to move the needle forward and why.

There's a myriad of things I do to feed my mind, but I never miss this step. It is important to always learn, stay grounded, and get in the right headspace. Lastly, I move my body to get the endorphins flowing. An added bonus is when you work out consistently you feel better about yourself. Other people will pick up on that confidence.

My Morning Routine

5:00am – Wake up, pray/meditate, stretch

5:10am - Brush teeth, wash face, weigh myself, drink 20 oz. of water

5:30am - Head to the gym, eat apple on the way

7:00am - Phone calls start for business on the East Coast, tend to calls and any missed messages, begin work day

Other Steps You Can Incorporate into Your Morning Routine

- Not hitting the snooze button
- Have coffee or tea
- Prepare a nutritious breakfast
- Say positive affirmations
- Listen to a podcast or YouTube
- Prioritize your tasks

While my morning routine may look pretty dialed in, that hasn't always been the case. It will take you some trial and error, but once you're in the flow you will immediately notice the difference in your days. Keep in mind, your routine may change during your career. Be malleable in your approach.

When I was doing more informational interviews to land a job, I set aside twenty minutes to figure out who I wanted to reach out to for an informational interview, or I took the time to make a list of people I needed to follow up with that day. When I realized my morning routine had such a huge impact on my productivity, I made sure to cut out any and everything that was not beneficial to me. While it may be difficult to cut out certain bad habits, the quicker you do the better off you are. When you become hyper-aware of how your actions and reactions affect you, you will notice certain bad habits that maybe you were unaware you even had. Sometimes we have been doing something for so long, we don't even take the time to step back and evaluate whether that activity is meaningful or not.

For me, that useless activity was answering or feeding into negativity before I completed the morning routine I set out for myself. For example, I realized some people in my inner circle always had a problem or needed my help as soon as I woke up. Trying to help people first thing in the morning and them not liking my solution or fighting with me was like dealing with leeches at the beginning of my day. I began to realize this often altered my mood negatively, had people relying on me more than they should've been comfortable with, and ultimately only hurt me. When I realized no one cared about how they were affecting me, I had to set boundaries. Now, if people call me with negativity or something non-urgent in the beginning of the day, I politely say, "I have a full schedule today. I will circle back with you later.

Have a great day." I keep it short and to the point. By doing this, the person knows that I have a lot on my plate, but that I am aware of the situation and will deal with it when time permits. For a while I was unaware others were eating into the most important part of my day. Mornings are typically the only time you can make for yourself, so be selfish and intentional with what you do in your waking hours.

Establishing a Nighttime Routine

Often overlooked, having a nighttime routine is just as important as having a morning routine. By creating a nighttime routine, it can make the morning routine and the next overall day smoother. I find having a nighttime routine helps me wind down and get organized, and frees up brain space so I can sleep better. If you have a big informational interview or any important meeting, having a nighttime routine can put your mind at ease and will most likely lead to better results. Since days can be hectic and overwhelming, especially when you've got a rigorous schedule, I recommend doing an activity to calm your mind and body, creating a plan for the next day, and trying to eliminate distractions as you get ready for bed.

My Nighttime Routine

9:00pm - Full body stretch post–hot shower, stretch
9:30pm - Write out a list of items I need to do tomorrow (business, personal, and miscellaneous)

9:45pm - Briefly journal about my wins for the day and what I could have done better

10:00pm - Put phone on do not disturb, lay out my workout and work clothes for the next day

10:30pm - Go to bed and meditate/pray

Other Steps You Can Incorporate into Your Nighttime Routine

- Read
- Bedtime tea
- Deep breathing (try the Wim Hof method or box breathing)
- Brief household cleanup

As you can see, a large part of both the morning and nighttime routines consists of eliminating distractions in order to reconnect with yourself. As you will see in the upcoming chapters, the tactical strategies of having informational interviews and making the most of them can be a tedious process. However, the more dialed in you are with your routine, the easier your day-to-day will become. What once seemed insurmountable will become your personal standard. Eliminate guesswork, create positive habits.

Prep Your Week

In addition to having a morning and nighttime routine, I recommend taking one day a week to prep for the week ahead. By knocking out your errands, cleaning your environment, and knocking out some of the monotonous tasks, you will be able to dedicate more time to focus on your goals. You don't need to brunch every Sunday or veg out on the couch for the entire weekend. When you fail to prepare for the week, it often leaves you making frantic choices and you end up having more personal tasks to tend to on a daily basis. Being strategic with your time will bring you peace of mind and enables you to get ahead of 90 percent of people.

My To-Do's Every Sunday
- Deep clean household
- Create next mini-goals for the upcoming week
- Go grocery shopping and meal prep
- Add all meetings and appointments for the upcoming week to my digital calendar/notebook

Other To-Do's You Can Incorporate Weekly
- Do laundry (sheets, clothes, towels, iron dress shirts)
- Go to a farmers market to buy fresh produce
- Wash your car
- Plan out your social media posts

As you can see, establishing proper habits doesn't have to be overly complicated. Implementing the right habits simply means mastering the mundane. Once you have a handle on all the items you know you need to get done, life's curveballs become more manageable. When you're building your personal habits, remember to move your body, clean your environment, eliminate as many day-to-day decisions as possible, feed your mind, and constantly revisit your goals along with the intention driving those goals.

Before you get into creating a new morning, nighttime, or weekend routine, it's imperative to take note of what you're doing now. In the checklist below, be diligent and honest about what your current habits are. After personally auditing your routines, you will be able to improve and build off of what's already working and get rid of any habits that may no longer be serving you. After the audit, take the time to build out new routines you want to commit to.

Current Morning Routine

Time	Current Habit	Beneficial (Y/N)

New Morning Routine

Time	Task

Current Nighttime Routine

Time	Current Habit	Beneficial (Y/N)

New Nighttime Routine

Time	Task

Current 1x/Week Prep Day

Time	Current Habit	Beneficial (Y/N)

New 1x/Week Prep Day

Time	Task

Apply It

Is there anyone you need to set boundaries with in order to focus wholeheartedly on yourself during personal time? Do you have time hijackers? Who are they? What do they repeatedly do? How will you set boundaries with them moving forward?

_____

_____

_____

_____

_____

_____

Make a list of habits you want to incorporate into your new morning routine.

_____

_____

_____

_____

_____

_____

_____

_____

_____

_____

Make a list of habits you want to incorporate into your new nighttime routine.

_____

_____

_____

_____

_____

_____

Make a list of tasks you want to complete once a week to make the rest of the week smoother.

_____

_____

_____

_____

_____

_____

_____

_____

_____

_____

_____

_____

_____

_____

Chapter 7

Getting the Informational Interview

"Each failure brings you one step closer to success."

Zig Ziglar

You've gained clarity on what you want to achieve and you have key mentors in place to help guide you along the way . . . now what? It's time for execution. The "doing" is usually the hardest part. More often than not, people will get excited and motivated once they have decided that they *want* to do something. But interest alone isn't enough. You can have numerous supporters rooting for you from family to mentors, but support means nothing if you never jump into action.

Once the initial excitement wears off, discipline must kick in. It will be an amazing view from the top of the mountain, but when you're at the base of that same mountain looking at the treacherous path up, you realize the trek will be arduous—and no one can climb it but you. Executing means simply placing one foot in front of the other. While executing seems simple, it can be extremely difficult to power through day in and day out. By continually doing what needs to be done, one day you'll be able to look up from that highest vantage point. With continuous execution, any goal is attainable.

Outreach

Once you have a general idea of what your next personal milestone will be (or at least you have an idea of who you want to meet with in order to gain more clarity) you need to begin making more connections through outreach. Although outreach can be intimidating, it is a fundamental part of landing more informational interviews. The more people you connect with, the better off you will be.

In graduate school, a professor of mine would repeatedly ask me, "What's more important, Henry—knowing your shit or knowing the right people?" Being the best at your job doesn't matter. Knowing the right people is the most important thing. Don't let anybody tell you differently. I beat out plenty of more qualified people, people who were "better" than me and smarter than me, because they did not know the right people or how to work the room. You can equate this to an underground artist. You could be great artistically, but if you do not know how to market yourself or connect with the right people, you might just be known as being the greatest basement player of all time.

Mutual Connections

The easiest way to establish new connections in order to set up informational interviews is through people you already know. When people say it's a "small world," it's true. The six degrees of separation theory states that all people in the world are connected by six connections or less. Even if this theory cannot be proven to be 100 percent true, if you think about the concept of a "friend of a friend," the sheer amount of people you are actually connected to, even if not directly, is astounding. Take full advantage of the mutual connections you already have.

Can your mentors connect you with more people who would be helpful for you to know? Before you get too in your head and automatically say no, be sure to ask. When you ask a mentor or a friend to connect you with someone, be sure that they are aware of the type of person you are interested in meeting. What industry are they in? Do they have a specific skill set? Do they have your dream job? Have they scaled a business so much so that you just want to pick their brain? The more information you are able to share with people who are well connected, the more likely they will be able to make valuable connections to help you.

Social Media and Email

As you know, you can find the majority of people (myself included) spending a considerable amount of time hyper-focused on their devices, aimlessly scrolling. Although social media can at times be a double-edged sword, when used the right way, social media can be a powerful tool to establish new connections. Prior to having social media, there was no real way to connect with people across all industries with the click of a few buttons. Consider yourself fortunate to be able to establish connections that would be next to impossible were it not for social media.

Before you begin to message people with the hopes of getting an informational interview, there's a few housekeeping items we must address:

1. Clean up your digital footprint and make sure your social media profiles are a positive representation of yourself. Yes, everyone has their vices—but they do not need to be plastered throughout your profile. If you are trying to land an informational interview with a professional in any industry, would they even want to give you the time of day?

2. Start building your social media profiles to reflect the job, business, and life you want to cultivate. By doing this, you may have like-minded people reach out to you without even asking! Always try to provide value on your social media profiles, even if you are starting small. Someone is always watching.

3. Show your personality! When you begin to show who you genuinely are, people will gravitate toward you.

My favorite social media platforms for outreach are Instagram and LinkedIn. After you find people you want to connect with, DM them (translation for anyone older than a millennial: send them a direct message). Introduce yourself. Your initial message should be no longer than five sentences. The main goal is not only to chat in messenger, but to get their email to set up an informational interview. While setting something up in person is always best practice, if they are located far away, a quick Zoom call will work too. If they are located in close proximity, you should always try to have the meeting in person. No matter how much you've grown accustomed to your home office, a face-to-face interaction will always take precedence over a video call.

Pro Tip

Instagram, LinkedIn, and email are gold mines for informational interview possibilities. Many people underutilize these tools. Make sure you maximize their features.

Here's an example of how to craft your initial DM:

Hello, Ms. Brighton.

I'm Henry Organ. I'm a communications major looking to land my first full-time position in public relations. I've heard people rave about the positive work your public relations firm helps facilitate within the community. If time permits, I'd love to have a quick fifteen-minute Zoom call with you to gain more insight into how I can land a job, or hear if you know of any paid internship opportunities. I've attached my reel so you can get a better sense of my work. My email is example@university.edu, I look forward to hearing from you.

Another example if you're an entrepreneur or business owner:

Hello, Mr. King.

I'm Henry Organ, founder of a tech startup. I recently came across your social media profile and love the neighborhood cleanups you have been organizing in the community. I have clients in your area who are all about giving back to the community. I think that there may be some synergy between us. If you have any availability next week, I'd like to schedule a quick fifteen-minute informational interview with you to pick your brain and learn about your business. Maybe we can throw an event together in the future. My email is example@company.com. I look forward to hearing from you!

On the contrary, here's a few examples of what NOT to do (and yes, these are people's actual attempts to set up an informational interview with me):

Example #1

Josh: What's up, Henry! We should connect...

Henry: Hey, Josh. Would love to connect. Send over an email with a little bit about what you do and we can schedule a time that works for us.

Josh: I really don't use my email very often. I only hop on phone calls.

Example #2

Hey fam. My name is Sam Smith. I'm based out of Miami and I am able to help get your clients the best marketing deals. I've seen a few paid ads your clients have done and the companies. Let me know if you are ready to get down and do business. Hit me up.

As you can see, even though both have made an effort to initiate contact, they were both rude and unprofessional. When you're asking for someone's time or looking to see if they can offer you an opportunity of any kind, be sure to always be courteous and professional.

Here are a few pro tips for social and email outreach you should try:

1.   **Instagram** - Search hashtags that are correlated to your job, industry, or business to find people to connect with. Start interacting with the profiles you find interesting by following them and commenting on posts that resonate with you.

Also, turn your profile into a business or content profile. This will enable you to have a "Primary" and "General" section in your DMs. Have your outreach under the "General" section so you will be able to keep it separate from your personal messages. This will help you stay organized and will make it easier to keep track of your business connections, without them being shuffled in the mix.

2. **LinkedIn** - Invest in LinkedIn premium. With LinkedIn premium, you can find numerous people across any industry. The awesome thing about premium is that you can run an in-depth search including specific company names, seniority levels, experience, and more. If you're frugal like me, give the thirty-day free trial a go and challenge yourself to make as many connections as possible. If you see an ROI in a month, keep it.

3. **Email** - If you want to connect with anyone, head to their company's website. You will usually be able to find contact information for employees. Email them your brief introduction and ask for an informational interview. If you're looking for a job, attach your résumé or portfolio and a cover letter. If you are an entrepreneur, aim to provide value in your initial outreach email. The name of the game is to get your foot in the door. Even if you cannot connect with the CEO or a higher-up employee, is there another angle you can take? Does the person you want to

connect with have an assistant? Can you send the assistant a small gift and request they schedule you for a fifteen-minute meeting?

Location, Location, Location

Another way to start meeting more people to start having more informational interviews is to get creative! Even though mutual connections and social media should serve you well if you heed the advice noted above, there are numerous other ways you can connect with people.

While strategically emailing people you want to connect with is a fantastic way to build rapport, don't be afraid to get back to the basics and introduce yourself the old-fashioned way, in person. You increase your odds of connecting with people you want to connect with by being in the right environments. People are willing to pay a premium to join social clubs and networking groups for a reason. Savvy people don't get fixated on the membership costs, they focus on the ROI the membership can provide.

I like to say "go where they go." Work from a coffee shop once in a while. If you overhear a conversation or you notice someone working on something that interests you, introduce yourself when they have a minute. Don't be shy! Also, make sure you always have a business card on you or something tangible you can give them to make them remember you. I handed out business cards before I even had a business. The cards just had my contact information, as seen below. Some of my friends laughed at me, but I didn't care. My goal was to connect with people and give them something they could take away.

If you're not comfortable meeting new people, getting creative with outreach can be difficult at first. However, the more you put yourself out there, the easier it becomes. Are you going to let being a little shy in the beginning get in the way of you reaching your full potential? If you want something as bad as you say you want it, you will be willing to get creative to make it happen. As soon as you proclaim you want something, life has a funny way of throwing curveballs at you. I believe various challenges emerge as a test. Do you just say you want it, or will you rise to the occasion and prove to yourself that you're committed to reaching your goals?

Sealing the Deal

When I was trying to land my first corporate job, I initially used mutual connections to help me seal the deal. When I made up my mind that I wanted to work in Nike Football, I did not know a single person who worked in that department. I had to get creative. I realized I potentially knew somebody who knew somebody who knew multiple people in that industry. Call it a small world, or the six degrees of separation, or simply my gut instinct, but I knew someone could help. I asked multiple people if they could assist in pointing me in the right direction.

Melanie Dixon was the director of the multicultural scholarship program at Portland State. She was also a diversity and multicultural scholar during my time as an undergrad there. She proved to me that mutual connections were powerful beyond comprehension. Since she gave me my scholarship, I had to report directly to her. I told her I wanted to work at Nike, and she connected me with her brother James Dixon, an actor and sales rep. James had nothing to do with Nike whatsoever, but he was well connected. James was able to introduce me to Anthony Herrington. Anthony spearheaded all of the supplies and logistics for Nike in North America. Anthony was a VP, but his job was nothing that I wanted to do whatsoever. However, he was the first president of the Black Employees Network.

Despite me not wanting to have a role similar to Anthony's, I knew the importance of nurturing that relationship. Anthony would give me the names of people to reach out to in pre-LinkedIn days. Anthony was a soundboard. In the grand scheme of things, you would think Anthony really didn't have shit for me—but because he was a director, he had hiring manager experience. When I applied for jobs, I asked him if he knew anybody in that field just as a friend. He may not have known that particular field at all, but he had friends in those divisions. He was able to point me in the right direction.

There were times when people would not give me an introduction, not anything. It was simply extra work for them. But all I needed was a name and an email address. I'd email that motherfucker myself and then name drop the person who wouldn't give me an introduction, like "so-and-so sent me."

A typical email from me would look like:

Hey Rodger,

Looking to see if you have 15 minutes for me to take you to coffee to conduct an informational interview sometime next week. I was referred to you by Anthony Herrington, who said you would be a great person to speak with about your journey to becoming a product line manager at Nike.

Short, simple, to the point. Boom. I'm in the door, I've already been vetted with Anthony's credibility. Or I'd email them and cc Anthony on it. In my Les Brown voice: "I was HOOONGRYYY." Physically, mentally, and spiritually.

I cannot stress this enough: ask to meet for fifteen minutes within the next week or two. For ease of scheduling and to eliminate back and forth you can say something like, "Please give me three times that work for you over the course of the next week and I promise to make one of them work." This creates flexibility but by making it timebound, it implies you have a sense of urgency. Do not say in the next month or whenever you have free time. Everybody has three times in the week that are open in their schedule, and if they don't they will have it the following week. If you get three people out of a hundred, you now have three new connections.

There will be times when you have to be fucking annoying. In one instance, I emailed a guy probably close to a hundred times to get the one interview that actually landed my first Nike HQ job. By the time the guy got back to me, he gave me an interview. Not an informational interview, an actual interview. Had I not been that consistent, I would've never been at the forefront of his mind as a potential candidate for hire when a position did become available. Later on he told me he admired my persistence; that was the main reason he set up a meeting with me in the first place. Because of all of the informational interviews I had, I was prepared to excel in the interview and received the job as Nike Football Brand Marketing Specialist.

To this day, I still have the emails I sent to him. Even after the first twenty emails, I never stopped. Below is an actual email I sent to him along with attachments of my project and résumé

From: **henry organ** <henry@example.com>
Date: Mon, Jun 2, 2014 at 7:48 AM
Subject: Relentless
To: M. Andy <example@nike.com>

Andy,

I know you are busy, but let me know if you have a minute to sit down for an informational interview. Below is a new concept idea that I came up with and have sent to the guys in FBAT.

The concept and idea was constructed through meeting with the Seattle Seahawks practice squad players at a training facility, and validated by focus groups of elite college football players at Oregon, Oregon State, and Portland State. Furthermore, it was then enhanced and endorsed by NFL Pro Bowler Julius Thomas.

As you can see, in order to seal the deal when scheduling informational interviews, persistence will be key. In retrospect, it's kind of funny that after not getting a response and sending a dozen emails, my subject line was "Relentless." Although I felt defeated at the time, I did not let my feelings get the best of me. My discipline kicked in and I continued to execute.

Please note, if you do not have a mutual connection with the person you are reaching out to, be sure to always add value and not only introduce yourself. You'll also notice I did not just say hello. I included a concept I thought would be beneficial to the person and the company they work for. From this, the person can automatically gather that I'm not just asking for a handout. Always aim to provide some sort of value from the jump. You must differentiate yourself from all the other general inquiries they get every day. Simply introducing yourself and asking for help is beyond unacceptable . . . it's flat out embarrassing! If you are going to shoot your shot, do so with pride.

Messages people will flat out ignore can look like the following:

- "Hey man, my name is Tom. I just graduated. Looking to connect to learn more about what you do."
- "What's up. I see you doing your thing on social. Let's link up. I have some ideas for you."
- "Hello. Can we schedule a phone call. I really want to chat with you."

Don't get me wrong, while brevity is appreciated now more than ever, it is still critical that you not only introduce yourself, but also include why you want to connect and provide some sort of value or insight so the receiver knows you're serious about establishing the connection. The people you are going to want to meet oftentimes value time more than money. Don't waste theirs or your own with subpar initial outreach efforts.

From: **henry organ** <henry@example.com>
Date: Thu, May 2, 2013 at 12:58 AM
Subject: Henry Organ (Portland State University Football)
To: Dan@shoecompany.com

Hey Mr. Frantz,

My name is Henry Organ. I met you several times in the past three years while I played football for Portland State University. I tested cleats and workout shoes, documenting hours and giving feedback about how they were. Michael, the Equipment Manager here at Portland State, gave me your email so I could get in touch with you. I am extremely passionate about Nike and your field of work. I aspire to work similar to yours and I thought that you would be a good person to connect with. I am just ending my junior year here at school and I would love to possibly acquire an internship with you or get any sort of work experience within the company, as it is my dream to do so. I am trying to get my foot in the door with Nike and will do so in whichever way possible. If you cannot help me, hopefully you can lead me in the right direction. I look forward to hearing from you soon. Thanks in advance.

Sincerely,
Henry Organ

Scheduling an informational interview is more than half the battle. In order to seal the deal, you must be willing to ask for the interview. While small talk is fine and dandy, you ultimately need to ask for what you want. Persistence speaks volumes about you. Even if no one is acknowledging it, people notice. People always quit if they don't get a response. People will always cry, saying, "I emailed him five times . . . I didn't hear back." Who gives a fuck! If someone doesn't respond to my email within the first week, I hit them up a week later. Then I hit them up every week thereafter and I set a time.

You can now schedule emails to go out in advance. Back in my day you had to log in and send the email. As a general rule of thumb, if you've never met the person before and are trying to get an initial response, follow up once a week for the first four weeks. The next month, follow up every two weeks. If they still do not respond, follow up once a month the third month. By month four, kick it up a notch and email them two days a week for a month straight. Month five, email them for the entire month. If you get no response, then and only then do you kill the deal and stop the outreach.

When asking to meet for an informational interview, always offer a small incentive for the other person to meet you. I'm not saying you have to take every single person out to lunch, but at least offer to buy them coffee. Make them feel like they got something in exchange for their time. Not having money is not an excuse. Sell a few of your material possessions. There was a point when I sold around thirty pairs of my shoes, not because I wanted to, but because I realized I only have two feet and I wanted to place more importance on my future.

If you're asking yourself: How do you get over thinking you're being obnoxious when you're doing outreach and asking to meet up? Don't be a wimp. If anyone is talking shit about you or has an issue with you, they'll respond to your email. If you happen to see them in person, remind them. "Hey man, I sent you an email, did you get it?" Don't be afraid to be that person. At one point in time they were in your shoes. Don't be a complete dick in person or in email, BUT don't be afraid to say, "Hey man, another email for you, I'm not giving up. Will you meet with me?" Address the elephant in the room. To this day, I know every single person who did not respond to my emails. It's crazy because I ended up becoming some of those people's boss or they eventually ended up needing things from me. I remember that shit. Again, don't be afraid. Make it awkward. Have them feel your presence. You got to have a lot of "fuck you energy." Controlled "fuck you" energy. Controlled "f**** you, motherf****, I emailed your ass and now I'm kicking your f******* ass in the workplace and doing big things" energy. Not in an arrogant way, but in an "I'll do whatever it takes" sort of way.

Believe it or not, the competition in the world is fierce. While you should only be competing with yourself, you've got to have a tenacious mentality. You've got to be like that because the competition thinks like that. I don't give a fuck what they tell you to your face. I don't give a fuck what they tell other people. When someone of importance is in the comfort of their own home, they have that fucking energy. You bought my book because you want to be somebody! You didn't buy this book to be the same. So forget what excuses you're making and follow my steps.

Apply It

Who in your network can you reach out to right now that may be able to connect you with the right person or people?

Reach out to the members of the Board from Chapter 4. Tell them what you are trying to accomplish and ask them to connect you with anyone who may be able to help you.

Review your social media platforms and make sure they are a good representation of who you are and what you want to become. If not, clean them up!

_____

_____

_____

_____

_____

_____

Once you've done a personal audit of your social media profiles, direct message at least ten people and introduce yourself. Have a goal of getting their email and scheduling at least one informational interview within the next two weeks.

_____

_____

_____

_____

_____

_____

_____

_____

_____

Once you've set up your first informational interview, document how many times you had to initiate contact prior to securing the meeting. This will help you realize the persistence it takes to schedule each informational interview moving forward.

Chapter 8

The Warm-Up

"The fight is won or lost far away from
witnesses—behind the lines, in the gym,
and out there on the road, long before I
dance under those lights."
Muhammad Ali

Details Matter

Once you've done the legwork, knowing what you want to
accomplish and who you can meet to help you get there,
it's time to knock every informational interview out of the
park. Like anything in life, preparation will be key to making
the most out of informational interviews. With every informational interview you have, the goal should be to leave
each person awestruck. By preparing for every interview,

you will exude confidence, and anyone you're meeting with will automatically pick up on the effort you've put in. Why would you go through all the trouble to set up an informational interview and drop the ball when it counts? If you've made it this far, it's your time to shine!

Your Highlight Reel

Prior to having an informational interview, prepare what I like to call a "highlight reel." A highlight reel in this context is an elevated résumé. If you can, create a portfolio that is a general synopsis of your journey. Oftentimes, people do better with visuals. If you have any notable projects you've worked on or something you can show them from your business, have it ready! I used to update my portfolio monthly. I would also keep a list of projects I was working on. From this, they were able to gather who I was and were able to provide feedback or figure out if they could help me in any way.

Always gear your visuals to who your audience is and what you are trying to sell. You are *always* trying to sell something. Don't ever forget that.

While I was trying to land a job at Nike HQ after undergrad, I created a portfolio to show everyone I had an informational interview with. At the time, my portfolio included projects I worked on, volunteering, potential ideas I thought I could implement if I was given the role I was working toward, and a thorough résumé On the next four pages, check out a few examples of what I included in my portfolio.

HENRY ORGAN

E-MAIL:
CELL:

PROFESSIONAL SUMMARY

Creative marketing professional with strong communication skills, including presentation, facilitation and vision execution. Extensive knowledge of the athletic industry and trends in the marketplace. Proven ability to translate former sales experience into successful nationwide marketing campaigns. Strategic thinker.

QUALIFICATIONS

- 3+ years' experience in consumer marketing and sports marketing.
- Ability to adapt in any environment.
- High level of proficiency with Microsoft Office, including Excel spreadsheets ,SAP ,SRM ,WebFlow

EXPERIENCE

SEPT 2015 - PRESENT | Focus Sports Agency | Beaverton, OR
EXECUTIVE BRAND DIRECTOR

SEPT 2015 | FOCUS SPORTS AGENCY

- Creation of Focus Sports Agency's creative content including: company logo, and website design, and prospective client presentation.Devising and executing strategic recruitment plans to sign prospective NFL athletes.
- Devising and executing strategic recruitment plans to sign prospective NFL athletes.
- Creation of marketing materials such as brochures and flyers to NFL teams to increase draft awareness.
- Cultivate existing and new relationships with strategic partners to develop our athletes' brands off the field.
- Increased ROI by 32% YTD

APRIL 2015 - PRESENT | Focused Models | Beaverton, OR
CEO/FOUNDER

APRIL 2015 | FOCUSED MODELS

- Provide the most qualified former and current athletes for digital advertisements, commercials and runway modeling for companies such as: Nike, Jordan, Riddell, Welch's, Strideline Socks, and more.
- Develop and maintain the front-end functionality of Focused Model's website.
- Created the company logo to elevate and differentiate branding and marketing initiatives.
- Negotiate compensation to secure maximum pay for models and recurring work.

SEPT 2014 - SEPT 2015 | Nike | Beaverton, OR
FOOTBALL BRAND MARKETING COORDINATOR

JULY 2015 | THE CRENAMO (NIKE)

- The Opening: Assisted in the execution of the Nike Opening, product shipments, and event execution.
- Nike Football Muse: Selected the muse for the Nike Football category in 2015 and facilitated briefing his story to the entire Football category, coinciding with our consumer experience journey.
- Gear Up: Assisted in idea creation and execution of the silos to help differentiate specific player's needs, in addition to execution of photo shoot needs.
- Madden 16: Initiated and implemented a collaboration of current Nike and Jordan football products being advertised in the game to increase product awareness and indirectly increase sales.
- Assisted in the first "Gear Up for Greatness" marketing campaign for the football category, which hosted 20 of Nike's tier one athletes in Las Vegas, NV.
- CFP: Executed the first ever College Football Play-off photo shoots and jersey unveiling.
- Responsible for all Football seasons' buys, inputs for the category, cross category and territories to ensure elevation of products in brand activations and incentives.

MARCH 2015 | GEAR UP (NIKE)

JAN 2015 | COLLEGE FOOTBALL PLAYOFFS (NIKE)

2014 | SONS OF THUNDER (HEART AND HUSTLE)

EXPERIENCE CONTINUED

SEPT 2013 - OCT 2014 | Nike | Beaverton, OR
NIKE COMPANY STORE ATHLETE

- Delivered brand expertise through consumer interaction, corporate storytelling, and knowledge of Nike products.
- Strategically drove business and achieved results through sales execution tailored to the consumer interests.
- Participated in all Nike EKIN University and attended all clinics.
- Selected as Nike Company Store MVP in June 2014.

2013 - 2014 | HEART AND HUSTLE PRODUCTIONS

JUNE 2013 - JUNE 2014 | Heart and Hustle Productions | Portland, OR
PRODUCER/TECHNICAL DIRECTOR

- Founded the creative idea board for projects included but not limited to: Ndamukong Suh documentary film, Portland Thunder Sports documentary film, and Nike BHM recap video.
- Coordinated production teams and assisted in establishing project visions.

2013 - 2014 | COCA-COLA

AUG 2013 - May 2014 | Coca-Cola | Portland State University
COKE BRAND MANAGER

- Ranked #2 in the nation for Coke Zero University promotional events and #5 in the nation for Diet Coke University promotional events.
- Successfully managed a team of 6 ambassadors who promoted Coke grassroots' marketing campaigns to elevate the brands of Coco-Cola, Diet Coke and Coke Zero.
- Executed promotional and consumer events, orchestrated social media outlets, and built partnerships with companies including: Spotify, Regal Cinema Rewards, and Portland State University Athletics.

2013 | PROCTER & GAMBLE

FEB 2013 - MAY 2013 | Procter & Gamble | Portland State University
P&G CAMPUS AMBASSADOR

- Recognized as the #1 student ambassador for Procter & Gamble in the Northwest and led Portland State University to place in the top 10 campuses nationwide.
- Promoted Procter & Gamble products to student communities through utilizing strategic marketing data and consumer analytics, generating brand awareness, brand trial activations and social media engagement.

EDUCATION

Portland State University, Portland, Oregon
Bachelor of Science, June 2014
Major: **Communications** | Minor: **Business**

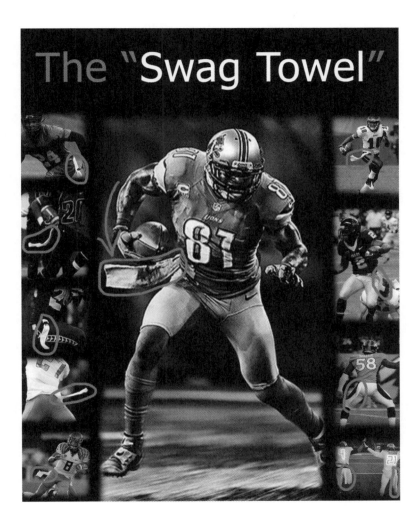

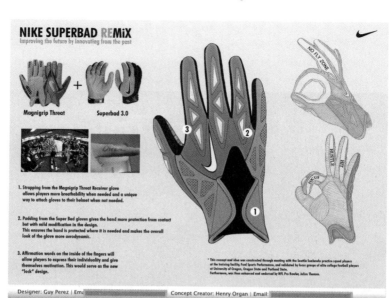

NIKE SUPERBAD REMiX

improving the future by innovating from the past

Magnigrip Threat + **Superbad 3.0**

1. Strapping from the Magnigrip Threat Receiver glove allows players more breathability when needed and a unique way to attach gloves to their helmet when not needed.

2. Padding from the Super Bad gloves gives the hand more protection from contact but with mild modification in the design.
This ensures the hand is protected where it is needed and makes the overall look of the glove more aerodynamic.

3. Affirmation words on the inside of the fingers will allow players to express their individuality and give themselves motivation. This would serve as the new "lock" design.

* This concept and idea was constructed through meeting with the Seattle Seahawks practice squad players at the training facility Ford Sports Performance, and validated by focus groups of elite college football players at University of Oregon, Oregon State and Portland State.
Furthermore, was then enhanced and endorsed by NFL Pro Bowler, Julius Thomas.

Designer: Guy Perez | Email: Concept Creator: Henry Organ | Email:

Role Play

Practice, practice, practice. Before you have an informational interview, you need to role play. By role playing, you are able to get clear on how to convey your message, to prepare for any questions the other person may ask you, and to think on your feet more quickly.

To make your role plays more realistic, do your research prior to your meeting. You can find out a lot about a person or an industry simply by Googling them. Once you find out a little more about the person or the company, you can tailor the conversation more toward their personal interests.

I typically role play with my girlfriend, mom, sister, dad, uncle, or even my fish. Repetition is key. There will potentially be a lot that you won't be able to foresee. You have to be able to adapt on the fly. If you practice enough, the conversation will be second nature for you by the time the meeting comes around. Role playing will also help you to avoid getting starstruck and freezing up in the moment. The conversation may not go as you imagined, but at least you practiced. Even if your informational interview does not turn out to be 100 percent what you had hoped, the other person will be able to tell you've made a determined effort.

Attire

While people nowadays are getting used to casual attire and working from home, make an effort to dress up, no matter if you are meeting in person or over Zoom. You still should aim to maintain work culture attire. Although it may not seem like a big deal, people forget that how you present yourself speaks volumes about who you are. Not to mention, when you look good, you feel good. When you feel good, you will perform optimally. I'm not saying you have to get a personal stylist. Don't overcomplicate it. Have a few go-to pieces for your informational interviews. Keep it simple, professional, and sharp. Since I don't like to overwhelm myself with choosing an outfit, I have outfits prepared even if I don't have anything scheduled. I created a professional, uniform look that I knew would work for any meeting. My go-to outfit for informational interviews was and still is a white button-up, black jeans, and comfortable sneakers. Streamline what you can.

Apply It

Prepare a one-pager for your next informational interview.

_____

_____

_____

_____

_____

_____

What projects have you worked on or are you currently working on that you can potentially bring with you? A thesis? A business plan? Something from a prior volunteer experience, internship, or job?

_____

_____

_____

_____

_____

_____

_____

_____

_____

_____

_____

_____

Write down a list of a few people you think would be good to role play with to prep for your informational interviews.

_____

_____

_____

_____

_____

_____

For each and every informational interview that you have, create an objective. Do you want to ask if they know of any job openings that you'd be a good fit for? Do you want to learn more about if they are satisfied with their job? Do you want them to potentially invest in your company? Do you want to bring up a business idea and make them aware that you think they'd be a great business partner for your future endeavors? Get to the root of what you are looking for out of each and every informational interview. While you role play, make it a point to get to your objective.

_____

_____

_____

_____

_____

_____

Figure out a few go-to outfits you already have that you think would be great to wear for your informational interviews. Bonus: Hang your picks in a specific area of your closet so they are easily accessible when needed.

Chapter 9

Gametime

"Ask for what you want and be prepared to
get it."
Maya Angelou

I t's gametime! By making your vision and objectives clear, seeking advice from mentors, and doing consistent outreach, you will surely land plenty of informational interviews. When it's time to meet up with someone you are interviewing, it is important to put your best foot forward. When it comes to informational interviews, since more often than not the interviews will be short in duration, it's vital that you make the most out of the time you do have with each and every person.

Now that you've done the prep, let's take a deeper dive into the actual interview. Eventually, having the informational interview will be the easiest part. The outreach, prep, and follow-up will account for most of the heavy lifting. But for the first few informational interviews you have, you may be a bit nervous. In order to calm your jittery nerves down, take a few deep breaths prior to the meeting and visualize the conversation flowing easily. You did your homework and now is when your preparation pays off.

The Beginning

First things first, make sure you show up to the informational interview at least ten to fifteen minutes before the scheduled time. When you're having the interview, make sure you keep it to fifteen, no more than thirty minutes. Some people are very diligent with their time. In the beginning, ask them how much time they have so you don't go over. Also mention that you realize their time is very valuable. Set your clock when you begin. Doing this shows you are mindful.

Your initial goal is to get the other person to talk about themselves. As they answer your first question, listen carefully. Be genuinely interested in their story. You want to find common ground with them before you speak about yourself and your main objective. Whoever asks the questions first controls the conversation. Smart informational interviewers will get the other person to talk about themselves right out of the gate. Your objective is to get them talking and to connect the dots to find commonalities to ultimately get them to see themselves in you.

The initial question doesn't have to be complex in order to find common ground. Try out the following:

- Where are you originally from?
- How did you get into this business?

If you couldn't find it online during your preliminary research, ask if and where they went to college.

When you do respond, take into account what they said. Did you also go to their college? Have you visited their hometown? Can you pick up on something else that they said? You can always find common ground.

Remember, only talk about the things that relate to them, don't just talk about yourself. Keep your elevator pitch short. No one cares about you. People have short attention spans. Make them see themselves in you. Find that one point they resonate with; see that in their eyes. Make sure they emphasize.

As soon as the opportunity presents itself, you also want to demonstrate that you have done your homework. You don't want to come across as uninformed after they've agreed to go out of their way to meet with you. Make a point to mention something early on regarding pertinent information you were able to gather online prior to meeting. By doing so, you will prove you aren't showing up to this meeting blindly. You are well prepared.

The Middle

After the early jitters are out of the way and the conversation is flowing, it's time to kick it up a notch. Hone in on the bulk of the questions you'd like answers to during the meeting. Focus on trying to make the other person see themselves in you. If you can get the other person to realize you have many similarities, they will become open to sharing more. I would advise you to ask your top two questions first in case the questions provoke in-depth answers. Keep in mind you may also have follow-up questions that pertain to how the person you're interviewing responds.

Your questions will be unique to your personal objective and what you're trying to achieve; however, if you're completely unsure of what to ask in order to reach your objective, feel free to take inspiration from the questions below and tailor them to fit your needs:

Newcomers and Career Swappers

- If you were going into this position blindly, what advice would you give yourself?
- What skills does it take for someone to thrive in your position?
- Are you happy with your career? If so, why?
- After this role, what's the next progressive step in your career?
- What are some of the benefits of this role and/ or industry? What are the potential pitfalls to consider?

- Do you know of any open positions that may be a good fit for me?

Corporate Ladder Climbers

- What experience do you need in order to thrive in your role?
- What do you think I can do in order to land a promotion faster?
- Are there any industry-specific books you've read that have drastically helped you with your career?
- How are you able to manage your workload as your responsibilities expand?
- Are you satisfied in your current role? What's next?

Entrepreneurs

- Why did you get into this business?
- How did you grow your team? When did you know it was time to scale?
- Has the team enabled you to grow your business faster?
- What's one of the biggest lessons you have learned about being an entrepreneur you wish you would have learned earlier?
- Where do you see yourself in the next five years?
- Is there anything I can do to help you? When you lead with help, your network grows (even if the industry they're in doesn't directly correlate with your business).

Figure out how to turn a business connection into a personal connection and in the end you or your business will reap massive rewards. Hint: Ask more personal questions in the informational interview and work to maintain the relationship.

The End

At the end of the interview, I suggest asking, "How can I improve my informational interview skills?" Regarding you as a professional or your business, "What are some areas that you think can be improved?" However they respond, be thankful for their insight. Remember not to take their observations personally.

Pro Tip
Failure is feedback.

Personally, there were many times when I did receive valuable feedback. Early on, in one of the first informational interviews I scheduled, I showed up empty-handed. The guy I spoke with asked me why I didn't bring a notebook. Honestly, bringing a notebook never crossed my mind because to me it wasn't a formal interview per se. To me, the informational interview was just to pick his brain and to see if he could help me. Big mistake. He also made me realize that bringing my résumé (what I now refer to as a one-pager) is important, even if it's not a job interview. It's an easy way for the other person to see your experience at a glance without eating into too much of the time you have scheduled to talk and to know that you're serious. From that point on I always asked for honest feedback. I would take bits and pieces of advice I received from each person. Each time I got better. I never stayed the same.

Miscellaneous Tips

When you have a meeting, there are a few other minute details you should be mindful of. They may seem obvious, but believe me, the vast majority of people are unaware.

- Never EVER show up late.
- Make sure your breath smells good, but don't chew gum. One of my favorite teachers of all time, Brother Kenneth, used to say, "When you chew gum, you look like a cow."
- Always bring a notebook. When you don't have a notebook, it basically tells the other person you're not *that* interested in what valuable information they have to offer. You aren't there to transcribe every word they are saying, but you need to jot down key points you don't want to forget.

During the conversation, look the person in their eyes when possible. If you're uncomfortable with eye contact, practice while role playing. Eye contact conveys attentiveness.

Following Up

Within twenty-four hours after the informational interview, send a follow-up thank you card or email with a thoughtful message. I usually send a coffee or smoothie gift card for $5 if I do not buy them coffee that day. Thank the person for taking the time to meet with you and also try to mention one piece of information you found invaluable. Not only will they love the gift card, they will love the fact that they were able to make a positive impact on you. If the informational interview went well, also ask if they can connect you with two more people that they think you should know. You will see a direct ROI for the time and effort you put into meeting with them. As your network grows, so will your opportunities.

If you take the follow-up process as seriously as you take the prep and the actual time you spend with that person, you never know what other opportunities or insights the person may provide even after the meeting is over. You never know if the person you've met has gotten a chance to go through their Rolodex to connect you with someone else, or if they've taken a liking to you and want to continue the conversation.

How you maintain relationships is just as important as making new connections. Brief informational interviews will never get you what you want if you fail to follow up.

Below is a real-life example of a response I received after sending a follow-up email thanking the person I met with for their time.

From: **Henry Organ** <henry@example.com>
To: O, Kim
Subject: Thank You | Henry Organ

Ms. O,

Thank you so much again for meeting with me as well as setting up the informational interview with Mr. Smith and Eric. I appreciate it. I am all about giving back as well so if there is anything I can do for you please don't hesitate to ask!

Henry

From: **O, Kim** <Kim@shoecompany.com>
To: Henry Organ <henry@example.com>
Subject: RE: Henry Organ

Hi Henry,

You are welcome. Hope you had a safe trip. I will set up an additional meeting for you with Derek Foster in Global Football Merchandising. Hopefully Mr. Smith and Eric will provide additional network opportunities for you. Dave P. mentioned that he gave you a temp agency contact. I am glad that he did. Please let me know if I can be of any additional assistance.

Thanks and Kindest Regards,
Kim

Apply It

Write down one icebreaker question that can be your go-to to get the person you're meeting with to talk about themselves.

_____

_____

_____

_____

_____

_____

If any of the suggested questions resonated with you, write them down. Do these questions spark any other questions you want to ask people in your informational interviews? What are they?

_____

_____

_____

_____

_____

_____

_____

_____

_____

_____

In your email or a blank document, create a templated "thank-you" email that you can send out after every informational interview. Of course this should be customized for each person, but having an email template ready to go will save you time.

Chapter 10

Tracking to Win

"When performance is measured,
performance improves. When performance
is measured and reported back, the rate of
improvement accelerates."
Pearson's Law

As you can see, informational interviews require quite a bit of leg work. From outreach to prep to the actual interview to following up, the overall process can be arduous, with many nuances, especially if you are coordinating a few informational interviews per month. As you complete your informational interviews, it is imperative to track your progress.

I suggest taking notes immediately after your informational interviews; if anything occurs post-interview as a result, track that as well. Keep one notebook for all interviews. By taking notes directly after each interview, you will be able not only to take note of what you learned from that person, but to use tracking as a means of evaluating your own performance.

I have always evaluated my informational interview skills. My goal when evaluating myself is to remain as objective as possible. If I was simply a fly on the wall making observations, what would I take note of? I've learned to use my deficiencies as building blocks to improve. I'm revisiting my pitch. I'm critiquing. I'm making adjustments. I'm not coming with the same exact energy every single time. For example, in one of my very first informational interviews the guy asked, "What else do you have for me?" I was drawing blanks. I had nothing. It was beyond embarrassing. The next time I came prepared with more questions. I already discussed the meeting in which the person (who was providing tremendous value) asked if I had a notebook to jot stuff down. Unfortunately, again, I was not as prepared as I thought I was. Ever since that interview, I've always brought a notebook. Even if you think an informational interview went well, you can always improve. Nobody's perfect. It's okay to acknowledge where you messed up. You are refining your skills.

It's equally important to acknowledge what you did right. Our minds can get fixated on what we did wrong. Your mind will automatically jump to what you coulda, woulda, and shoulda said. But what about the things that went right? Did the conversation flow nicely? Did you get the answers you were looking for? Were they able to connect you with people who can potentially help you in the future? Did you improve on something you messed up in a previous informational interview? Remember to give yourself credit when credit is due! The more informational interviews you do, the easier the process will become.

- Like I said, I recommend tracking your progress in one place. Keep a list of people you met with in a notebook or a Google Sheets file. Track your performance per month. How many informational meetings have you had? Who did you meet with? What was discussed? Some columns I personally keep in my Google Sheet include:
- Name/Role + Company
- Email
- Date I Met w/ Them
- Thank You Note Sent? (Y/N)
- Key Takeaways
- What Went Wrong
- What I Did Well
- Who They Connected Me With

Miscellaneous Notes

By having my notes in a single document, not only am I able to see how much my interpersonal skills have improved, I'm also able to retroactively look back and see how informational interviews have helped propel my career and business forward. Having this information documented encourages me to keep scheduling more informational interviews, even when I don't feel like it.

Tracking will help sustain the connections you've worked so hard to get. If you're looking for a job, don't be afraid to circle back with someone even if you haven't spoken with them in a while. If you are searching for a job at their company and something sparks your interest, hit the person back up. Let them know once you've applied to the role. Maybe they will even put a good word in for you. You may even be able to get more information from them. Ask them questions like:

- Can you tell me who the best person is to contact regarding this position?
- Has this role already been filled?
- Do you have someone internally who is filling the role?

If you're an entrepreneur, don't be afraid to circle back with your Rolodex of contacts either, even if you haven't spoken to them in a while. If you ever need a vendor or think someone you've met in the past can help your business, don't be afraid to ask. Your notes will refresh your memory regarding who may be able to assist you and in what way. I also suggest sending a brief "checking in" email to all of your contacts every quarter so they will keep you top of mind for any potential business opportunities.

I have an additional list of every single person who told

me what I couldn't do. I've met over 100 people. I've emailed over 200 people. Most never responded. Sometimes it serves you to have a chip on your shoulder. It's okay for you to keep a list of people who told you no or simply never responded. It's okay to feel like you don't want to continue. It's okay to feel like you're annoying. You are most likely annoying.

Embrace all of it. Be a dog. Be a lion. Be a champion. You're going to be great regardless because most people are scared to do any of this, period. The beautiful thing about informational interviews is that you're not competing with anybody but yourself. You're not doing push-ups or lifting weights, you are literally talking to people.

Pro Tip

The more at-bats you have, the higher you increase your chances of succeeding. People get defeated by doing the same thing and not getting results. Tracking will help you critique your at-bat.

By tracking your progress, you will be able to stay focused on both your immediate and long-term goals. Like anything else, consistency will be key. You will begin to recognize patterns that have the power to showcase where you struggle and also what may come naturally to you. Besides helping you strategize to improve for future networking opportunities, seeing how far you have come will encourage you to keep going when you may feel defeated. Having your tracking sheet for reference will instantly empower you.

The book is your coach. Tracking will be your version of watching film. How many other people can say they are meeting up with people, tracking their key takeaways, and constantly looking for ways to improve? I can tell you now, the average person isn't doing that shit. You're not an average Joe though, or you wouldn't still be reading this to learn how to separate yourself from the pack. Schedule the informational interviews, track your progress, and make it habitual. Your life will improve tenfold and others will begin to ask you: how do you know so many people? How did you accomplish so much in such a short period of time?

Apply It

It's time to create your own tracking sheet! Make it in Google Sheets or Excel. Copy my columns Date, Name/Role + Company, Contact Info, Thank You Note Sent? (Y/N), What Went Wrong, What I Did Well, Who They Connected Me With, Key Takeaways, and Miscellaneous Notes.

Tracking Sheet Example

I've created an example tracking sheet from pages 142 to 145. I have nine column headers (see pages 142 and 144), but your columns can be unique to how and what you'd like to track. This is just a snapshot so you can have an idea. Use my blank template on page 146 to get started. Eventually your tracking sheet will have numerous contacts and notes to pull from.

Date	Name/Company and Role	Contact Info	Thank You Note Sent (Y/N)	What Went Well	What Needed Work
9/8/22	Erin/Shoes Inc./ Director of Communications	erin@example.com	Y	I was able to find common ground fast. He loves football like me.	I wasted too much time with banter. I forgot to limit the chitchat and clearly go over my objectives.
9/15/22	Ashley/Compass/ Product Specialist	ashley@example.com	Y	I got her to talk about her career in depth and what the reality of her job is. I did not even know product specialist was a job!	I did not do my best with telling her about myself. I realized my elevator pitch needs work. I need to communicate my strengths.

9/28/22	Kai/Web Developer/Ayo Startup	kai@example.com	N	I was more comfortable in the conversation. I let him talk and clearly conveyed my strengths.	I did not research the startup enough. I wasted time asking questions I should've already known the answer to (like what the company was about).
10/1/22	Mark /Social Media Manager/Time Magazine	mark@example.com	Y	I was not so rigid with my conversation. I listened to what he was saying to ask the next question, not just what I had initially planned on asking him.	I did not take notes. I was so wrapped up in what he was saying, I completely forgot some of the details I wish I could've remembered.

Who Did They Connect Me With?	Key Takeaways	Miscellaneous
Did not ask them to connect me with anyone else!	Mutual ground is great but keep the conversation focused.	Remember to arrive early, Erin was early and although I was on time I felt rushed since he beat me to our meeting location.
Alex, a marketing manager @ Compass!	There are more career paths that may be right for me that I'm simply unaware of.	We went to the same high school

Tony UI/UX designer	I do NOT want to be involved with overly technical career paths, despite the high pay.	He might be a great contact to help build my website if I ever start my own business. He mentioned he also runs his own business on the side and helps small business owners. Remember to send him a holiday card.
Forgot to ask	I would highly consider doing what Mark does! He truly seems fulfilled with what he does on a daily basis. We seem to have a ton of the same interests.	There's a company holiday mixer he invited me to. Email him closer to the beginning of December to get the details.

Date	Name/Company and Role	Contact Info	Thank You Note Sent? (Y/N)	What Went Well?	What Needed Work	Who Did They Connect Me With?	Key Takeaways	Miscellaneous

Chapter 11

Implementation

"Nothing in this world can take the place
of persistence. Talent will not; nothing is
more common than unsuccessful men
with talent. Genius will not; unrewarded
genius is almost a proverb. Education will
not; the world is full of educated derelicts.
Persistence and determination alone are
omnipotent."
Calvin Coolidge

Whether it be mastering informational interviews or succeeding in life, implementing what you learn and being persistent will be instrumental to your success. You must be relentless in everything that you do.

Whether that's during the initial stages of outreach or

asking for the help that you need, nothing is going to be given to you. Everything you get will be earned.

Mindset

Sometimes it will feel like you're losing. It will feel like you flat out suck, despite all the work you may be putting in. When you keep taking L's, you must keep a positive attitude. Make it a point to keep up your positive energy. When you are holding informational interviews, people will feed off whatever energy you are putting out. It's a fact.

To keep a positive mindset I keep quotes all around the house. Even on the days I don't believe the quotes ring true, the positive messages plastered on my wall do something to my brain.

My quotes read:
- "Your business is thriving!"
- "You're going to get a job."
- "You're sexy as fuck."
- "No one outworks you."
- "Life doesn't happen to you, it happens for you.
- "If you don't stay up all night, I will beat you."

There's a whole bunch of BS you can tell yourself, but at the end of the day, being positive is a choice. You are either positive or you're not. If you believe you can do it, you will. If you believe you can't do it, you won't.

I like to compare the similarities between myself and someone I admire to make me realize they are not "better" than me. A lot of times when people have their dream job, or own a big business, you think they are special or supernatural. I'm here to tell you that they're not. They've just had more failures than you. They've had more repetition. Think about the first time you tried to ride a bike without training wheels and saw other people riding it with ease. You probably were thinking: *WOW! How do they get to ride a bike with no training wheels?!* Then once you got the hang of riding a bike, you realized that riding a bike isn't that hard. They aren't a superhero, they're just like you. That's life! The more people you meet, you'll realize you're closer to your version of success than you may think.

I want you to be skeptical of everything you see. The vast majority of people do not show all of their late nights, early mornings, and mundane day-to-day sacrifices. Stop comparing your situation to someone else's achievements. What can look like someone's day 1 is really their day 10,000. I say all this to say: if you have goals you want to achieve, stop comparing yourself to others and get to work. Achieving anything in your life will take a tremendous amount of dedication. As much as everyone loves instant gratification these days, the loftier the goal, the longer it will take. Your life is a marathon, not a sprint. If you were asked to keep a sprinter's pace for 26.2 miles, do you think you'd be able to sustain it? Absolutely not. There are always techniques you can incorporate to cut down your time in a realistic way, and that's hopefully what this book has taught you. Being strategic and properly preparing for your race is ultimately what will cut down the time it takes to reach your goals.

Capitalize

For all the work that goes into informational interviews, be sure to capitalize on the connections you've made. I use informational interviews to this day. As I've mentioned, I'm able to utilize informational interviews in my business by growing my team and creating powerful connections that help my business grow exponentially. Relationships are the backbone of any business, and for that reason, I will never stop having them.

Pro Tip

Don't talk about what you're going to do . . . go do it!

In any field, you want to continue to grow your network because your network is your net worth. I challenge you to think about how you can use informational interviews to get whatever it is that you want. How will you get to the next step? How will you extract what you need from each and every interaction? How will you cultivate the relationships you build to gain more opportunities?

At the end of the day, there are talkers and there are doers. You can only pick one.

Apply It

List quotes you can put in a visible place that will inspire you to be persistent.

_____

_____

_____

_____

_____

_____

How can you implement the strategies in this book to help you level up in the coming months?

_____

_____

_____

_____

_____

_____

_____

_____

_____

_____

_____

_____

_____

_____

Email me to share your success stories and how informational interviews have helped you: info@disruptivesports.com

_____

_____

_____

_____

_____

_____

_____

_____

_____

_____

_____

_____

_____

_____

_____

_____

_____

_____

_____

_____

_____

_____

_____

_____

_____

Big Ideas

Use this section to write down your biggest takeaways and
ideas.

Appendix

Henry's book recommendations to help you along your journey:

1. *The 48 Laws of Power* by Robert Greene
2. *Principles* by Ray Dalio
3. *Believe to Achieve It* by Howard White
4. *Shoe Dog: A Memoir by the Creator of Nike* by Phil Knight
5. *Rich Dad Poor Dad* by Robert Kiyosaki
6. *Wooden on Leadership* by John Wooden
7. *Emotional Intelligence 2.0* by Jean Greaves and Travis Bradberry
8. *The Compound Effect* by Darren Hardy
9. *The Alchemist* by Paulo Coelho
10. *Creative Visualization: Use the Power of Your Imagination to Create What You Want in Your Life* by Shakti Gawain

Acknowledgments

"Once it's in your mind, nobody can take it away from you."
Claude Organ

I want to dedicate this book to the people who believed in me when many did not and wrote me off as average!

To my mother, Annette Devine; my godmother, Gayle Day; Aunt Julie Quin; and my aunt Noralee (Straw) Alexander.

To my grandfathers, William Devine and Claude Organ, MD, and grandmothers, Claira Polk and Elizebeth Organ, and my uncles, Eric Devine, Greg Devine, Paul Organ, MD, and Henry P. Organ.

To my friends: Taylor Martnick, Jerrel Jones, Mario Brown, Patreece Carson, Vanessa Nutters, Big Al, Taylor Tailulu, DeShawn Shead, Gee Scott Sr., and Adam Snyder.

To my teachers at St. Marys High School: Brother Kennethl, Mr. Puck, Jay Lawson, Adolph Bertero, Carol Balding,

Amy Gonzales, and Peter Imperial, and my teachers at St. Pauls High School: Mr. Young, Ms. Grossman, Keenan Miller, and Mr. Gordon.

To my mentors: Ray Anderson, Melinie Dixon, James Dixon, Anthony Herrington, Les Green, Rami Jabaji, Andy Miguel, Mark Chan, Aaron Goodwin, Cliff King, Aaron Woods, Timo Porotesano, PS Styles, Alanzo Carter, and Rashad Floyd.

To my schools: St. Pauls and St. Marys, Portland State and the Diversity and Multicultural Center at Portland State University, and the University of San Francisco sports management program.

To my previous employers: MAC Computers, Ace Hardware, Coca-Cola, P&G, and Nike.

To my business partner, Hector Rivas, and all of the founding clients of Disruptive: Kendrick Bourne, Brennan Scarlett, and Samori Toure.

To my publisher, Naren Aryal, CEO Of Amplify, who published this book after more than twenty publishers told me it would never work, and Myles Schrag, my project manager!

To my girlfriend, Cody Sims, who pushed me to write this book and stayed on me for two years to keep fighting to complete it.

I learned a great deal from all of these people along the way about how to master the informational interview and it inspired me to write this book.

To the underdog who nobody believes in: KEEP FIGHTING! WE BALL!

About the Author

Henry Organ is an NFLPA-certified sports agent who represents some of the most notable names in football. In addition to advocating for players on and off the field, Organ is a seasoned real estate investor and entrepreneur. Previously, he worked in brand marketing at Procter & Gamble, Coca-Cola, and Nike, and was producer and technical director at Heart and Hustle Productions. Organ graduated from Portland State with a degree in communications and a minor in business and obtained his master's in sports management from the University of San Francisco. Organ attributes the majority of his success to mastering the informational interview early in his career.